KU-537-791

Kingfisher
Encyclopedia
of
Lands & Peoples

7

ASIA

Kingfisher

General Editor Sue Grabham
Senior Co-ordinating Designer Tracy Killick

Editors Claire Berridge, Jane Butcher,
Charlotte Evans, Nina Hathway, Ann Kay,
Linda Sonntag, Jill Thomas
Assistant Editor Julia March
Editorial Assistant Virginie Verhague

Cartographer Alan Whitaker
Cartographic Editors
Tara Benson, Annabel Else
Assistant Cartographic Editors
Nicola Garrett, Victoria Hall
Cartographic Services
Cosmographics, Lovell Johns Ltd
Base Map Artwork Malcolm Porter

Senior Designer Janice English
Designers Paul Calver, Dawn Davies,
Earl Neish, Andy Stanford
Additional Design Branka Surla, Smiljka Surla

Additional Art Preparation Shaun Deal,
Roy Flooks, Mark Franklin, Matthew Gore,
Mel Pickering, Janet Woronkowicz

Writer Linda Sonntag

Picture Research Su Alexander, Elaine Willis
Artwork Archivist Wendy Allison
Assistant Artwork Archivist Steve Robinson

Publishing Director Jim Miles
Art Director Paul Wilkinson

Production Manager Linda Edmonds
Production Assistant Stephen Lang

Indexer Hilary Bird
Glossary and Phonetics Daphne Ingram
Proofreader Penny Williams

Geographical Consultants
Keith Lye, Dr David Munro
Natural History Consultant
Michael Chinery
Social Geography and History Consultant
Professor Jack Zevin

KINGFISHER

An imprint of Larousse plc
Elsley House, 24-30 Great Titchfield Street, London W1P 7AD

First published by Larousse plc 1995

Copyright © Larousse plc 1995

All rights reserved. No part of this publication may be reproduced, stored in a
retrieval system or transmitted by any means, electronic, mechanical, photocopying
or otherwise, without the prior permission of the publisher.

A CIP catalogue record for this book is available from the British Library

ISBN 1-85697-420-0

Colour separation by Newsele s.r.l. Milan, Italy
Printed in Italy

7

ASIA

USING THE MAPS

The box below contains a map key. It explains what the different symbols on the maps in this encyclopedia mean. For example, a square marks a capital city and a black line marks a road. On the right is a sample map. The lines of latitude and longitude are marked in degrees. The letters and numbers between the lines are the grid references. They help you to find places on the map by identifying the square in which they are found.

The scale bar on a map helps you to measure distances. On this map 2.2 centimetres equals 200 miles and 1.4 centimetres equals 200 kilometres.

The town of Antserañana is marked by a circle. The circle is in grid reference B1. To find it, all you have to do is look down the map from B and across the map from 1.

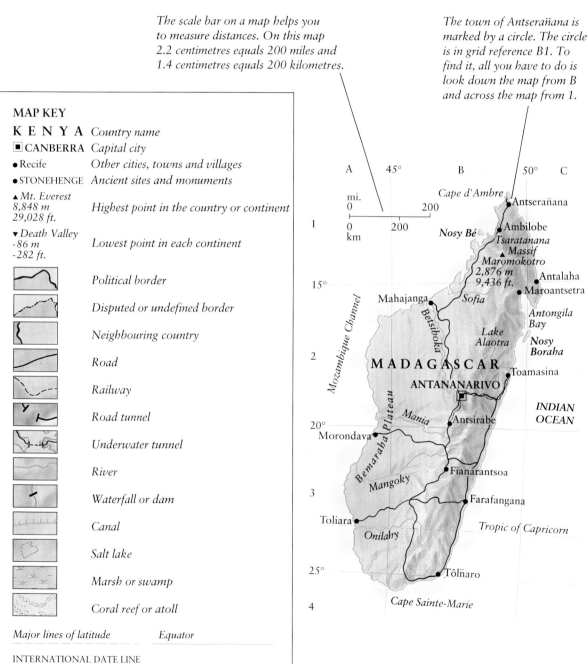

MAP KEY

K E N Y A   *Country name*

■ CANBERRA   *Capital city*

● Recife   *Other cities, towns and villages*

● STONEHENGE   *Ancient sites and monuments*

▲ Mt. Everest
8,848 m
29,028 ft.   *Highest point in the country or continent*

▼ Death Valley
-86 m
-282 ft.   *Lowest point in each continent*

Political border

Disputed or undefined border

Neighbouring country

Road

Railway

Road tunnel

Underwater tunnel

River

Waterfall or dam

Canal

Salt lake

Marsh or swamp

Coral reef or atoll

Major lines of latitude   *Equator*

INTERNATIONAL DATE LINE

ASIA

Arctic Circle

Tropic of Cancer

Equator

Tropic of Capricorn

ASIA *Geography*

Asia is the largest continent in the world, covering almost one third of the Earth's total land surface. It is part of the same landmass as Europe and stretches from Africa and Europe in the west to the Pacific Ocean in the east. Chains of volcanic islands mark the continent's eastern border, which is a danger zone for earthquakes.

Asia's northwestern borders are formed by the steep crags of the Ural and Caucasus mountains. Lands in the far north extend above the Arctic Circle, where much of the region is tundra – a frozen, treeless wilderness that is locked in ice for many months each year. Farther south lies a broad belt of evergreen forest known as taiga, which in turn gives way to open, fertile grasslands in the west and east. However, few rain-bearing winds reach Central Asia, so deserts have formed in this region. Little grows on the sandy wastes and barren, rocky plateaus where it is bitterly cold in winter and as hot as a furnace in summer.

The great triangular peninsula of India stretches south into the warm Indian Ocean. The world's highest mountain ranges, the Himalayas and Karakorams, form a barrier of ice and snow in the north. South of the mountains the snow melts into rivers that run through broad plains. These rivers often flood and deposit fertile soil over a wide area.

Asia's sunny southwestern coastline is washed by the Red Sea and the Mediterranean, but the lands and islands of southern Asia have a tropical climate. There, it is hot and dry for part of the year, but drenched by rain during the summer months. At this time stormy winds called monsoons gather up moisture from the southern oceans and shed it over the land.

▼ *The world's highest peak is Mount Everest* (left). *This snowy giant is in the Himalaya Mountains, which lie along the border between China and Nepal.*

◄ *Rice has been grown on these irrigated hillside terraces in the Philippines for 2,000 years. It thrives in the hot, monsoon climate of Southeast Asia and is the continent's most important food crop.*

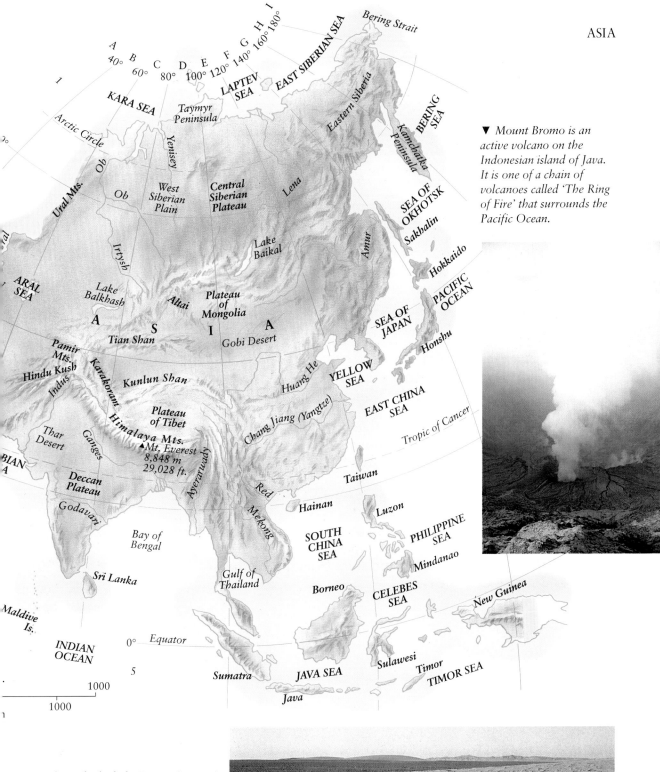

A B C D E F G H I
40° 60° 80° 100° 120° 140° 160° 180°

Bering Strait

KARA SEA

LAPTEV SEA

EAST SIBERIAN SEA

Taymyr
Peninsula

Arctic Circle

Eastern Siberia

Kamchatka
Peninsula

BERING
SEA

Ob

Yenisey

West
Siberian
Plain

Central
Siberian
Plateau

Lena

SEA OF
OKHOTSK

Sakhalin

Ural Mts.

Ob

Irtysh

Lake
Baikal

Amur

Hokkaido

ARAL
SEA

Lake
Balkhash

Altai

Plateau
of
Mongolia

PACIFIC
OCEAN

A   S   I   A

SEA OF
JAPAN

Pamir
Mts.

Tian Shan

Gobi Desert

Honshu

Hindu Kush

Karakoram

Kunlun Shan

Huang He

YELLOW
SEA

Indus

Plateau
of Tibet

Chang Jiang (Yangtze)

EAST CHINA
SEA

Thar
Desert

Himalaya Mts.
▲Mt. Everest
8,848 m
29,028 ft.

Tropic of Cancer

Ganges

Ayeruwaddy

BIAN
A

Deccan
Plateau

Red

Taiwan

Godavari

Mekong

Hainan

Luzon

Bay of
Bengal

SOUTH
CHINA
SEA

PHILIPPINE
SEA

Sri Lanka

Gulf of
Thailand

Borneo

Mindanao

Maldive
Is.

CELEBES
SEA

New Guinea

INDIAN
OCEAN

0°   Equator

Sulawesi

Timor

TIMOR SEA

5

Sumatra

JAVA SEA

1000

Java

1000

▼ Mount Bromo is an
active volcano on the
Indonesian island of Java.
It is one of a chain of
volcanoes called 'The Ring
of Fire' that surrounds the
Pacific Ocean.

► The Rub al Khali (Empty Quarter)
is a sandy waste stretching across
Saudi Arabia. The sand has been
shaped into rippled hills, called
dunes, by the wind. These dunes
change their shape as the wind blows.

ASIA *Political*

Some of the world's first great civilizations sprang up in Asia from 3500BC onwards. Their riches attracted trade and conquering armies. Over the centuries peoples such as the Mongols and the Turks built up and then lost vast empires. From the 1800s much of Asia was colonized by European countries. These new rulers took away wealth, but did not help the colonies develop their industries.

Great social changes have taken place in Asia during this century. Many colonies freed themselves from their European rulers, creating independent nations such as India and Jordan. In countries where a large majority of poor people were ruled by a wealthy few, communism seemed to be the answer. Communist governments set prices for goods and labour. They also owned all property. The idea was that people would share the profits as well as the work. However, the spread of communism often caused wars with capitalist countries where individuals were able to own property and to set all prices. In 1991 the Soviet Union abandoned communism and, as it broke up, republics such as Kazakhstan and Uzbekistan became independent countries. Some Asian countries still have communist governments, although a number have recently held democratic elections for the first time.

Many Asian governments are now improving the economies of their countries by creating new industries and improving old ones. They are using both government money and foreign aid.

▶ *Election posters line the streets of Lahore in Pakistan. After long periods of military rule Pakistan has become a democracy. The people now vote to choose a government.*

▲ *Mikhail Gorbachev was the leader of the communist Soviet Union. He brought in many reforms before the Soviet Union collapsed and he lost power in 1991. Since then the republics of the Soviet Union have become independent nations.*

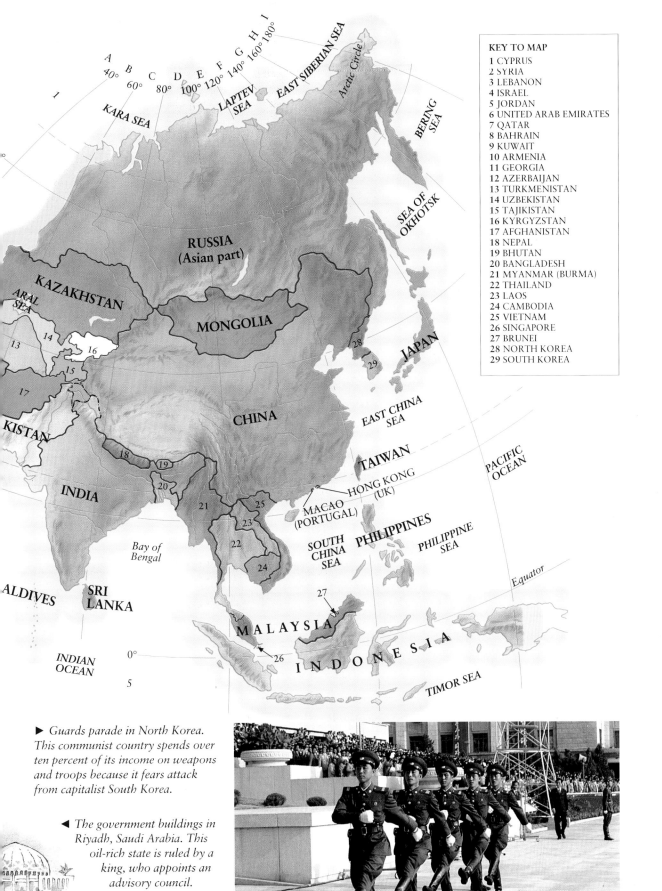

KARA SEA

LAPTEV SEA

EAST SIBERIAN SEA

Arctic Circle

BERING SEA

SEA OF OKHOTSK

RUSSIA
(Asian part)

KAZAKHSTAN

ARAL SEA

MONGOLIA

JAPAN

EAST CHINA SEA

CHINA

TAIWAN

PACIFIC OCEAN

HONG KONG (UK)

MACAO (PORTUGAL)

INDIA

PHILIPPINES

PHILIPPINE SEA

SOUTH CHINA SEA

Bay of Bengal

...KISTAN

...ALDIVES

SRI LANKA

INDIAN OCEAN

Equator

MALAYSIA

INDONESIA

TIMOR SEA

KEY TO MAP

1 CYPRUS
2 SYRIA
3 LEBANON
4 ISRAEL
5 JORDAN
6 UNITED ARAB EMIRATES
7 QATAR
8 BAHRAIN
9 KUWAIT
10 ARMENIA
11 GEORGIA
12 AZERBAIJAN
13 TURKMENISTAN
14 UZBEKISTAN
15 TAJIKISTAN
16 KYRGYZSTAN
17 AFGHANISTAN
18 NEPAL
19 BHUTAN
20 BANGLADESH
21 MYANMAR (BURMA)
22 THAILAND
23 LAOS
24 CAMBODIA
25 VIETNAM
26 SINGAPORE
27 BRUNEI
28 NORTH KOREA
29 SOUTH KOREA

► Guards parade in North Korea. This communist country spends over ten percent of its income on weapons and troops because it fears attack from capitalist South Korea.

◄ The government buildings in Riyadh, Saudi Arabia. This oil-rich state is ruled by a king, who appoints an advisory council. There are no political parties.

389

ASIA *Plants and Animals*

Thousands of the world's most beautiful plant species originally came from Asia, including tulips from Turkey and rhododendrons from the Himalayas. Other Asian plants have become valuable food crops. Rice was once a wild grass that grew in many of the continent's flooded river valleys.

Animals of all shapes and sizes are found throughout Asia. They include the Asian elephant, the Bactrian camel and the giant panda. The world's largest and smallest bats are also found on this continent. The tiny Kitti's hog-nosed bat lives in caves in Thailand, while the large Bismark flying fox is found in Indonesia. In the waters off southern Japan lurks the giant spider crab with a massive claw span of up to four metres.

Some of the most densely populated areas on Earth are found in Asia. To make room for fast-growing cities and industries, forests have been cleared, swamps drained and rivers dammed. This has often caused great damage to the nearby countryside. There has also been serious pollution, over-hunting and over-fishing. Some traditional Asian medicines include ingredients such as powdered rhinoceros horn and gall bladders of bears, so many animals have been killed to supply the trade. However, great efforts are now being made to ensure that no more animals are put in danger.

▲ *The caracal is a medium-sized desert cat related to the lynx. It was once found over large areas of the Middle East and India, but has become increasingly scarce.*

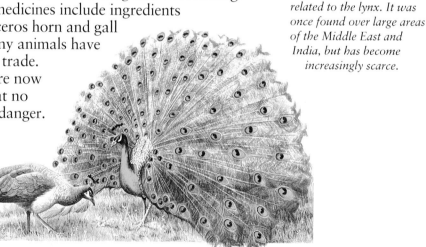

▶ *The male peacock fans out his tail to impress the female, a peahen. Peafowl are native to India, Sri Lanka and Southeast Asia.*

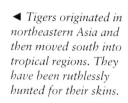

◀ *Tigers originated in northeastern Asia and then moved south into tropical regions. They have been ruthlessly hunted for their skins.*

▶ *The Arctic hare lives in the far north. In winter its brown or grey summer coat turns white to conceal it against the snow.*

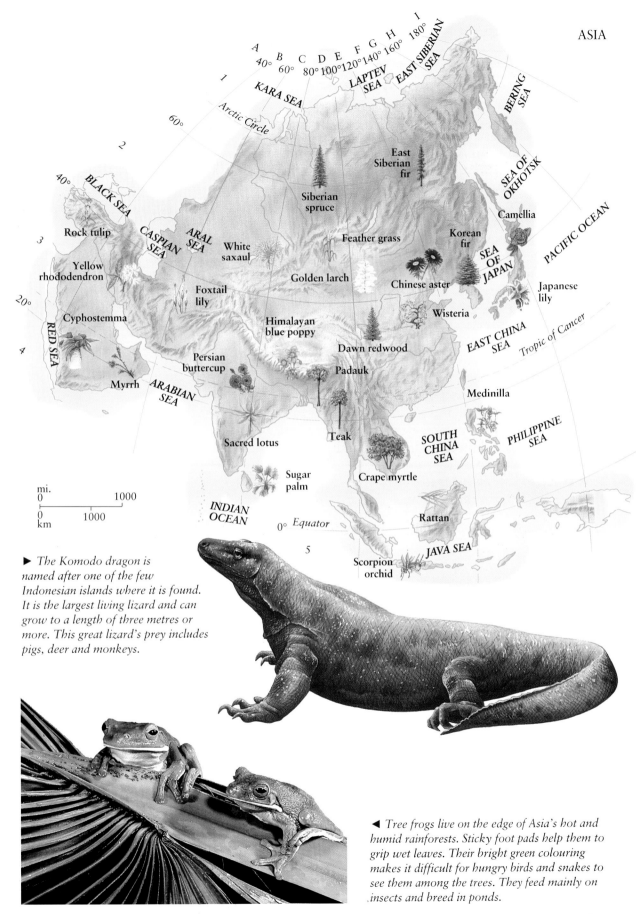

A B C D E F G H I
40° 60° 80°100°120°140°160° 180°

KARA SEA
LAPTEV SEA
EAST SIBERIAN SEA
BERING SEA

1

Arctic Circle

60°

2

East Siberian fir

Siberian spruce

SEA OF OKHOTSK

40°

BLACK SEA

Rock tulip

CASPIAN SEA

ARAL SEA

White saxaul

Feather grass

Korean fir

Camellia

PACIFIC OCEAN

3

Yellow rhododendron

Golden larch

Chinese aster

SEA OF JAPAN

Japanese lily

20°

Cyphostemma

Foxtail lily

Himalayan blue poppy

Wisteria

RED SEA

4

Persian buttercup

Dawn redwood

Padauk

EAST CHINA SEA

Tropic of Cancer

Myrrh

ARABIAN SEA

Medinilla

Sacred lotus

Teak

SOUTH CHINA SEA

PHILIPPINE SEA

mi.
0   1000

0   1000
km

Sugar palm

Crape myrtle

INDIAN OCEAN

0° Equator

Rattan

5

JAVA SEA

Scorpion orchid

▶ The Komodo dragon is named after one of the few Indonesian islands where it is found. It is the largest living lizard and can grow to a length of three metres or more. This great lizard's prey includes pigs, deer and monkeys.

◀ Tree frogs live on the edge of Asia's hot and humid rainforests. Sticky foot pads help them to grip wet leaves. Their bright green colouring makes it difficult for hungry birds and snakes to see them among the trees. They feed mainly on insects and breed in ponds.

RUSSIA *Introduction*

Russia is the largest country in the world. It covers over 17 million square kilometres, borders 14 other countries and crosses eight time zones. Extending north to the frozen wastes that lie above the Arctic Circle, its expanses also take in vast forests, high mountains and wide plains. Russia has long, bitter winters and short summers. Snow can cover more than half of the country for six months a year, so it can be difficult to make the most of the many natural resources available. These resources include large regions of farmland and plentiful reserves of timber, oil, coal, natural gas and minerals.

For centuries Russia was a vast empire ruled by emperors called tsars. However, a workers' revolution in 1917 eventually ended the reign of the tsars and brought the Bolsheviks (later called the Russian Communist Party) to power. Russia became a republic and in 1922 joined with three smaller republics to form the Union of Soviet Socialist Republics (USSR), also known as the Soviet Union.

By the 1940s the four original republics had been further subdivided and there were 16 republics in the Union. Over the next 40 years individual republics made increasing demands for independence. The USSR eventually broke up in 1991 and communism collapsed.

ENDANGERED WORLD

The musk deer is hunted because the male secretes musk, a scent that is used in the perfume trade. It lives in the forests of Siberia.

FACTS AND FIGURES
Area: 17,075,000 sq km
Population: 148,366,000
Capital: Moscow (8,957,000)
Other major cities: St Petersburg (5,004,000), Novosibirsk (1,446,000)
Highest point: Mt Elbrus (5,642 m)
Official language: Russian
Main religions: Christianity, Islam, Judaism
Currency: Rouble
Main exports: Natural gas, petroleum, chemicals, machinery, timber, coal, food
Government: Federal republic (transitional)
Per capita GNP: US $2,680

▲ *Kolominskye village is on the West Siberian plain. Despite Siberia's large reserves of oil and gold, few people live in this vast region because of its bitterly cold and long winters.*

▼ *Red Square is in Moscow, Russia's capital. On the left are the onion-shaped domes of St Basil's Cathedral. On the right is the Kremlin, which was originally built as a fortress. The Kremlin became the government headquarters under communist rule.*

► *The Trans-Siberian Railway offers the world's longest train journey. It takes about seven days to travel the 9,000 kilometres between Moscow and Vladivostok.*

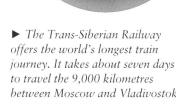
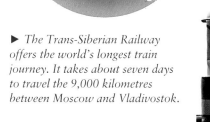

RUSSIA *Geography*

Most of this enormous country lies on the Asian continent, but western Russia is in Europe. The Ural Mountains are usually considered by geographers to form the dividing line between European Russia and Asian Russia.

Russia's climate includes great extremes, growing steadily hotter towards the south and colder and drier towards the east and north. As the climate changes, so does the landscape. Tundra covers much of the most northerly region. Little grows on this frozen plain and relatively few people live there. Only hardy animals such as reindeer and Arctic foxes can survive the bitterly cold temperatures.

Below this region a belt of dense forest sprawls across the country. Taiga, which is the name for forest made up of coniferous trees, makes up the northern part of the belt. The soil is mainly too poor to grow crops. Farther south the forest becomes a mixture of coniferous and deciduous trees. The climate in this region is milder and some areas can be farmed.

Rolling plains known as steppes start below the forests. Meadows and wooded plains make up the northern steppes. The southern steppes are mainly treeless, but their rich soil makes this some of the best farmland in the whole country.

The Caucasus Mountains and the shores of the Caspian Sea form Russia's southernmost area. The slopes of the Caucasus Mountains have lush, green, fertile meadows, while the Urals contain important deposits of iron and copper.

▼ *An ice-breaker works a passage through the floes on the Kara Sea. These vessels play an important role in a country where sea and river transportation is hampered by ice for much of each year.*

◄ *Lake Baikal is the deepest lake on Earth and contains more fresh water than any other. There are many species of plants and animals, including the Baikal seal, that are unique to the lake and its surrounding area.*

◀ The Indigirka River runs through the Russian taiga. This is a belt of spruce, fir, larch and pine forest that stretches across northern Russia. The region is also home to bears, elks and wolves. Under the trees is a scrubby growth of bushes that include crowberry, cowberry and bilberry.

▶ The Caucasus Mountains stretch from the Black Sea to the Caspian Sea. Spectacular glaciers and volcanic formations are found throughout the range. The Caucasus region is rich in mineral resources. There are oilfields and rich deposits of manganese.

◀ Hot water springs called geysers send up clouds of steam in Geyser Valley on the Kamchatka Peninsula. This region of active volcanoes juts out between the Sea of Okhotsk and the Bering Sea.

395

RUSSIA *Economy*

When communism ended here, with the break-up of the Soviet Union in 1991, Russia's economy had to make the huge and very difficult change from communism to capitalism. The word soviet means a council elected by the people and the basis of communism was that everybody should share both the work and the profits. Communist law stated that the government of the Soviet Union owned all the country's factories and farms as well as controlling everyone's wages and the prices of goods. Any profits were shared by the people and no one was allowed to run a private business. From the 1920s onwards communist Russia became a heavily industrialized nation. The government set up large factories and mines all over the country. Huge state farms were created and farming practices were modernized with the use of pesticides and fertilizers to increase yields.

After communism collapsed government price controls were lifted. Producers could suddenly charge what they liked for goods and prices soared dramatically. However, incomes remained very low and this caused great economic problems. Shortages were just as common as they had been under communism, partly because of the lifting of price controls. Today heavy industry, farming and mining are still extremely important and new ways are being found to exploit Russia's mineral resources. Service industries are also being developed.

▲ *Shoppers jostle each other to buy goods on the black (illegal) market. Under communist rule buying and selling was strictly controlled, but people with money were able to deal privately.*

▼ *Fishermen lift their catch out of the water. Ice covers many Russian lakes in winter. Holes are cut into the ice for fishing nets and the fish are carried home by sled.*

▲ *Combine harvesters work the fields on a collective farm. Under communism a collective farm is government-owned, but worked by people who share the profits. Though the growing season is short and rain is scarce, Russia's vast areas of farmland make it one of the world's major grain producers.*

▲ *A worker in Siberia checks oil-extracting machinery. Russia has large reserves of both oil and natural gas in Siberia and new fields are still being opened up. However, outdated equipment means that oil production is far less efficient than it could be and new investment in this industry is badly needed.*

ECONOMIC SURVEY

Farming: Most land is still government-owned, but private farms are being set up. Major crops are barley, flax, fruits, oats, potatoes, rye, sunflower seeds, wheat, sugar beet and vegetables. Forestry and fishing are important.

Mining: Russia has huge reserves of coal, oil and natural gas. It is also a major producer of gold, iron ore, lead, nickel, manganese, tungsten, tin and zinc.

Industry: Under communism the government owned all manufacturing plants and heavy industry took priority. Since 1991 consumer goods have increased in importance. The government is also working to convert the country's government-owned properties to private ownership.

RUSSIA *People*

The majority of Russians are descended from a people called Slavs, but there are small numbers of about 100 other ethnic groups. These include Ukrainians, Jews, Belarussians and Armenians. Most Russians live in European Russia, in the west of the country. Inuits are among the groups in the frozen far north. People in different areas feel strongly about their own identity. Some former Russian republics became independent in 1991 and there are still people in parts of Russia who would like total independence. One such area is Chechnya, with its capital at Grozny, where a revolt broke out in 1994.

Three quarters of the population lives in towns and cities. Russian cities have huge populations, so many people live in crowded, high-rise apartment blocks. Moscow has one of the highest population counts in the world – over eight million people have made their homes here.

During the years of communism education was made a top priority by the government, but religious worship and freedom of speech were severely restricted. With the end of communism Russians began to worship more openly.

Russia's strong artistic tradition has produced many famous writers, composers, artists and musicians. From the 1800s onwards the country was a world leader in literature, drama, music, ballet and other arts. It has also become a leading medal-winner in the world of sport. This is actively encouraged by the government, which provides a wide range of sports facilities such as stadiums, recreational centres and athletics clubs.

BORSCHT
Borscht is a classic Russian soup. There are many different recipes, but one brightly coloured favourite has beetroot as its main ingredient. This dish is eaten cold in summer and hot in winter. Sometimes meat or wild mushrooms are added. Barley is also used to thicken it.

▼ *In Siberia these Yakut and Khant women are making traditional clothes. Today these are worn only by rural people on special occasions.*

SPEAK RUSSIAN

Hello – Здравствуйте
(*zdras - vid - ye*)

Goodbye – До свидания
(*dah - svee - dahn - ya*)

Please – Пожалуйста
(*pah - zahl - sta*)

Thank you – Спасибо
(*spa - see - ba*)

Yes – Да (*dah*)

◀ These buildings are part of Moscow University. It was founded in 1755 and is Russia's oldest and largest university. Many teenagers go on to higher education. There are about three million students at the country's 500 colleges and universities.

▶ Stars of Moscow's Bolshoi ballet dance in a scene from Swan Lake. Russian ballet became internationally famous in the 1800s and the Bolshoi is still famed for its performances of the great Imperial Russian ballets of that era, such as Sleeping Beauty and The Nutcracker.

◀ These beautifully painted wooden dolls are traditional Russian toys. They are called matruschka (little mother) dolls and each one contains a series of smaller dolls inside it.

RUSSIA *History*

Balkan people were living in Russia around 1200BC and by the AD800s Slavs had settled here. Mongols invaded in 1237 and Russia was part of the Mongol empire for 200 years until a long line of Russian rulers called tsars began their reign. From the 1600s to the 1800s discontent with the tsars erupted into revolts. By the early 1900s revolutionary groups had emerged and in 1917 a group called the Bolsheviks led a revolution, under Vladimir Ilyich Lenin. Tsar Nicholas II was killed and Lenin set up a communist government, forming the Union of Soviet Socialist Republics (USSR).

Lenin's successor, Joseph Stalin, ruled by terror from 1929 until 1953. He was followed by less oppressive leaders such as Khrushchev, Brezhnev and Kosygin. The 1940s to the 1980s marked a period of distrust between the West and communist countries in the East, which is often called The Cold War. When Mikhail Gorbachev became president in the 1980s he introduced reforms that gave the people greater freedom. At this time some republics began to demand independence. By the early 1990s most of the republics were part of a Commonwealth of Independent States. Boris Yeltsin became Russia's new president.

YURI GAGARIN
The Soviet astronaut Yuri Gagarin became the first man to travel in space in 1961, when he orbited Earth in the satellite *Vostok I.*
The orbit took 89 minutes and was a triumph for the Soviet Union. It had beaten the United States of America in the race between the two countries to be first to put a man in space.
In 1963 the Soviet Union also put the first woman in space, Valentina Tereshkova.

◄ *Women march banging empty pots in protest against food shortages. After the collapse of the Soviet Union in 1991 state subsidies were stopped so the price of food went up. The end of communism has not brought improvements for everyone.*

▶ *Russia's president, Boris Yeltsin, came to power after Gorbachev resigned in 1991. Under Yeltsin's leadership most of the former members of the Soviet Union formed the Commonwealth of Independent States (CIS). The CIS is a group of independent countries with economic and defence interests in common.*

▼ *The Winter Palace in St Petersburg, built in 1732, was the winter home of the tsars. In 1905 thousands of striking workers marched to the palace to demand reforms from Tsar Nicholas II. Hundreds were killed by the Tsar's troops and the event became known as Bloody Sunday.*

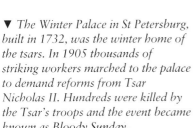

◀ *A Palm Sunday Parade gathers in front of St Basil's Cathedral (left) in Moscow. The cathedral was built during the 1550s by Tsar Ivan IV, famous for his fearsome temper, brutal behaviour and absolute power over the Russian people.*

GEORGIA

FACTS AND FIGURES

Area: 69,700 sq km
Population: 5,471,000
Capital: Tbilisi
(1,283,000)
Other major city:
Kutaisi (235,000)
Highest point:
Mt Shkhara (5,201 m)
Official language:
Georgian
Main religions:
Christianity, Islam
Currency: Lari
Main exports: Food,
chemicals, machinery,
metal products
Government:
Republic
Per capita GNP:
US $850

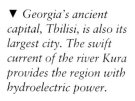

▼ Georgia's ancient capital, Tbilisi, is also its largest city. The swift current of the river Kura provides the region with hydroelectric power.

Although most of this country is in Asia, part of northern Georgia is in Europe. Forested mountains cover much of the land and snow stays on the highest peaks all year round. However, near the Black Sea the mountains' lower slopes are lush and fertile. These areas, along with the coastal lowlands, have a mild climate and plenty of rain, enabling farmers to grow citrus fruits, tea and tobacco. Farther inland cereals and vegetables are grown, as well as grapes for Georgia's famous wines. Georgia is noted for its food and hospitality and for the health resorts along its Black Sea coast.

Georgia was established as a separate region around 500BC, at a time when the ancient Greeks had settled here. It has been fought over by the Romans, the Persians, the Arabs and the Turks, but enjoyed a golden age of science and art under Queen Tamara (1184-1213). Since then arts such as music, opera and poetry have continued to flourish. The country also has its own language and alphabet. Georgia gradually became part of the Russian empire during the 1800s. In 1936 it joined the Soviet Union. Georgia became independent in 1991 and the early 1990s saw conflict between the country's different ethnic groups. In 1993 Georgia joined the Commonwealth of Independent States, the group of former Soviet Republics.

More than half of Georgia's people live in urban areas and many work in food processing, the country's main industry. Most of the population are Christian and belong to the Georgian Orthodox Church.

▶ *This church at Ananuri, just east of Tskhinvali, was built in 1689. The fortifications protected it from the Turks and Iranians, who were fighting over Georgia at the time. Christianity came to Georgia in the AD300s.*

▼ *For centuries shaggy sheepskin hats have been worn by Georgian shepherds and other rural people. They are said to keep the wearer's head cool in summer as well as warm in winter.*

Map of Georgia

40° A 43° B 46° C

Gagra

RUSSIA

Mt. Shkhara
▲5,201 m
17,061 ft.

1 Sukhumi

Caucasus

Ochamchira

Inguri

BLACK SEA

Zugdidi

Kutaisi

GEORGIA

Mts.

Poti

Tskhinvali

Alzani

42° Zestafoni

Khashuri

Kura

Telavi

Ozurgeti

Iori

Batumi

Akhaltsikhe

TBILISI

Rustavi

Little Caucasus Mts.

2 TURKEY

ARMENIA AZERBAIJAN

mi.
0 — 100
0 — 100

◀ *Georgian horsemen play a form of polo known as tskhenburi. The game of polo originated in Persia in about the 500BC and was brought to Georgia by Persian invaders. Polo is still a very popular sport and most towns in Georgia sponsor a polo team.*

403

ARMENIA

Armenia is a rugged country in the Little Caucasus Mountains, with deep gorges, lakes and rushing rivers. The earliest peoples were probably farming the land around 6000BC. Ancient Armenia was once a powerful independent kingdom. After defeat by the Romans in about 55BC it became part of the Roman empire. Later it was conquered by Arabs and Turks. Between the 1890s and the end of World War I the Turks massacred more than half a million Armenians and others were deported or fled. Over the years people from Armenia have settled in many other countries. Today there are millions of Armenians living all over the world.

Modern Armenia is only the northeastern part of the old kingdom of Armenia. The Russians captured this area from the Turks in the 1820s and it later became a republic of the Soviet Union. Armenia gained independence in 1991. The rest of historic Armenia is now largely part of Turkey. From the late 1980s there has been a dispute between Armenia and its neighbour Azerbaijan over the ownership of Nagorno-Karabakh. This area, in the southeast of Azerbaijan, is inhabited mainly by Armenians.

Most Armenians were farmers or herders until ruled by the Soviets. The Soviets set up copper mines and factories and many Armenians moved to the cities to work. Today only a third of the population is rural, keeping sheep or cattle and growing fruit and vegetables. Most people speak the Armenian language, which is unlike any other and has its own alphabet. The country also has a strong artistic tradition that includes religious music and the making of decorative stone carvings called *khatchkars*.

FACTS AND FIGURES
Area: 29,800 sq km
Population: 3,732,000
Capital: Yerevan
(1,283,000)
Other major city:
Gyumri (120,000)
Highest point:
Mt Aragats (4,090 m)
Official language:
Armenian
Main religion:
Christianity
Currency: Dram
(rouble also still in use)
Main exports:
Chemicals, food
products, machinery,
transport equipment,
metal goods
Government:
Republic
**Per capita
GNP:**
US $780

◀ *Geghard Church perches against a rock in the gorge of the Garny River, southeast of Yerevan. Armenia was the first country in the world to make Christianity its official religion.*

Map labels:
A 44°   B   46° C
GEORGIA
mi.
0   50
0   50
km
Alaverdi
Stepanavan
Spitak
Gyumri
Kirovakan
Dilizhan
Mt. Aragats
4,090 m
13,419 ft.
Sevan
Razdan
Lake Sevan
AZERBAIJAN
Echmiadzin YEREVAN
A R M E N I A
40° Aras
Vardenis Mts.
TURKEY
Ararat
Arpa
Goris
AZERBAIJAN Kafan
Mountains
Aras
IRAN

AZERBAIJAN

In Azerbaijan the lofty Caucasus Mountains sweep down to the Caspian Sea. The small area of the country north of the Caucasus is considered to be part of Europe, but the remainder of Azerbaijan is in Asia. In the southwest a corridor of Armenian territory separates one section of Azerbaijan, called Nakhichevan, from the rest. Much of the land is mountainous and through the broad valleys run the Kura and Aras rivers, which provide hydroelectric power for industry and irrigation for farming.

The people, called Azeris, are descended from a mix of Turkic peoples and Persians that were living in this area around AD1200. By the 1800s Russia was in control and Azerbaijan was part of the Soviet Union until the Union broke up in 1991. The Russians brought industrialization and today the economy is based on Azerbaijan's large reserves of oil and natural gas. There are also many factories and over half the people live and work in towns and cities. In rural areas farmers grow cotton, fruit, tobacco and tea. Sheep, cattle and goats are herded on the mountain slopes.

Ownership of the Nagorno-Karabakh region has been challenged by Armenia and there has been bitter fighting since the late 1980s.

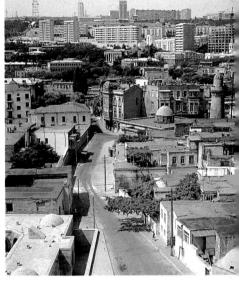

▲ *Baku, the capital, is Azerbaijan's major trading port and the centre of the oil refining industry.*

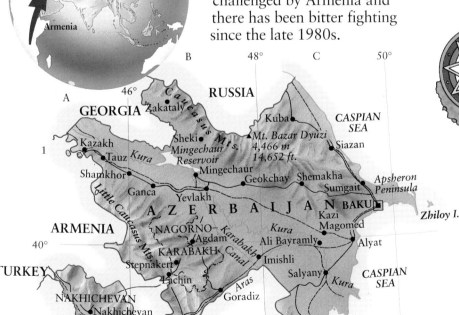

FACTS AND FIGURES
Area: 86,600 sq km
Population: 7,392,000
Capital: Baku (1,081,000)
Other major city: Ganca (283,000)
Highest point: Mt Bazar Dyuzi (4,466 m)
Official language: Azeri
Main religions: Islam, Christianity
Currency: Manat (rouble also still in use)
Main exports: Chemicals, food, machinery, oilfield equipment, petroleum, natural gas, textiles
Government: Federal republic
Per capita GNP: US $870

KAZAKHSTAN

ENDANGERED WORLD

The snow leopard has been hunted almost to extinction for its fur and only survives high in the mountains.

From west to east, the country of Kazakhstan stretches from the salty Caspian Sea to the soaring Altai Mountains. In the north are high, grassy plains called steppes and in the south there are arid, sandy deserts. Kazakhstan has bitterly cold winters and long, hot summers.

The Kazakh people are descended from the Turkic and Mongol invaders of the past. For centuries they were nomads, roaming the plains with their herds of camels, horses, sheep and cattle. The animals provided meat, milk, wool and even an alcoholic drink called kumis, made from fermented mare's milk.

This traditional way of life began to change when Russia conquered Kazakhstan about 100 years ago. Thousands of Russians settled here and today over a third of the population is of Russian origin. The Russians began to mine iron and lead. They also planted the Kazakhs' grazing lands with wheat. This process continued after Kazakhstan became part of the Soviet Union and rapid industrial development also took place. Many Kazakhs left their nomadic way of life and settled in villages, although a few still live in the old way. Traditional livestock herding continues, but many people now work on modern farms and their produce contributes greatly to the country's economy.

The years of industrialization and intensive farming have left pollution problems and many people in rural areas still live without electricity or running water. However, the discovery of oil in the Caspian Sea promises wealth and independence in 1991 brought a new sense of pride in the Kazakh language and traditions.

FACTS AND FIGURES
Area: 2,717,300 sq km
Population: 16,956,000
Capital: Almaty (1,151,000)
Other major cities: Qaraghandy (609,000), Shymkent (439,000), Semey (345,000)
Highest point: Mt Tengri (6,398 m)
Official language: Kazakh
Main religion: Islam
Currency: Tenge
Main exports: Oil, metals, chemicals, grain, wool
Government: Republic
Per capita GNP: US $1,680

▶ *Women on horseback look after their flocks of sheep. The tent, called a yurt, is traditionally used by Kazakh nomads. Some Kazakh villagers live in yurts today and herd livestock as their ancestors have done for generations.*

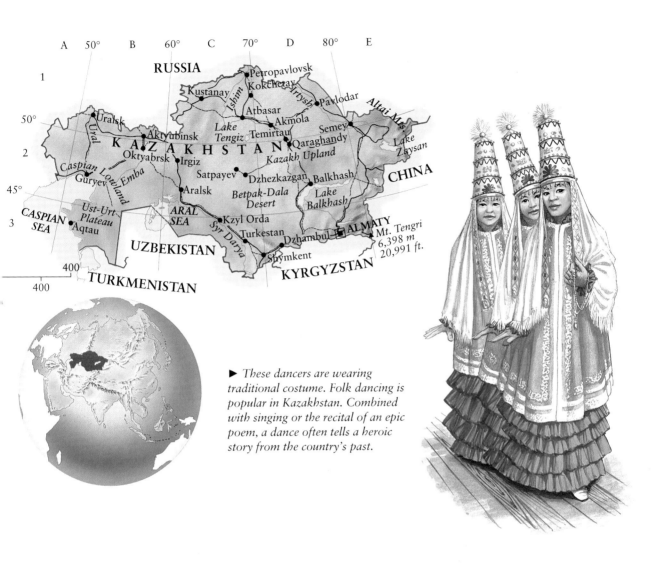

▶ These dancers are wearing traditional costume. Folk dancing is popular in Kazakhstan. Combined with singing or the recital of an epic poem, a dance often tells a heroic story from the country's past.

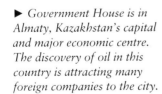

▶ Government House is in Almaty, Kazakhstan's capital and major economic centre. The discovery of oil in this country is attracting many foreign companies to the city.

407

TURKMENISTAN

Few people live in the arid desert region of Karakum that covers most of Turkmenistan. The inhabited areas of the country are mainly along the foothills of the Kopet Mountains in the south and in the river valleys of the southeast. Half the population of Turkmenistan makes its living from farming, which would be impossible without the canals that bring water from the rivers to irrigate the land. The most important crop is cotton, but grain, potatoes and grapes are also grown. Thoroughbred Turkomen horses and karakul sheep are reared and some farmers also breed silkworms. Wool is woven into the highly colourful carpets for which this country is famous.

The very first people to have lived in Turkmenistan may have wandered the deserts with livestock or farmed the more fertile areas. Turkic peoples made their home here around AD900 and controlled all or part of the area on and off until the 1800s. Russia invaded in the 1870s and from 1924 to 1991 Turkmenistan was a republic of the Soviet Union.

About 70 percent of the country's present population are ethnic Turkmen. They are Sunni Muslims and are descended from the first Turkic settlers. Family life is important to these people and several generations of a family often live together.

◀ A Turkmen woman works at the loom, weaving a carpet. Turkmen carpets are known for their strong colours and bold designs.

FACTS AND FIGURES
Area: 488,100 sq km
Population: 3,809,000
Capital: Ashkhabad (411,000)
Other major citiy: Charjew (166,000)
Highest point: In the east (3,137 m)
Official language: Turkmen
Main religion: Islam
Currency: Manat
Main exports: Consumer goods, food, machinery, metals, oil, natural gas, cotton, textiles, chemicals
Government: Republic
Per capita GNP: US $1,270

UZBEKISTAN

Much of Uzbekistan is a land of rolling plains and barren deserts, with the huge desert of Kyzylkum at its centre. Streams flowing from Kyrgyzstan's mighty Tian Shan Mountains water the fertile, heavily populated valley that contains the town of Fergana.

Uzbekistan is on the ancient Silk Road. For over four centuries, up until the 1400s, this was an important trade route from China to the Middle East. In about 300BC the region was conquered by the Greeks under Alexander the Great. By the AD600s the Arabs had invaded, bringing their religion of Islam. They were followed by the Mongols in the early 1200s.

Most of the people are Uzbeks, who are descended from a mixture of Turkic groups and other peoples including Mongols. There are also several minority groups, the largest being Russians. Russia conquered Uzbekistan during the 1800s, then in the 1920s the country became a republic of the Soviet Union. Uzbeks are nomadic herders by tradition, but the Soviet Union turned much of the country's grazing land into cotton plantations and the Uzbek people began to work on these. When the Soviet Union broke up in 1991 Uzbekistan became independent. It then joined the Commonwealth of Independent States, the association of former Soviet republics.

FACTS AND FIGURES
Area: 447,400 sq km
Population: 21,207,000
Capital: Tashkent (2,120,000)
Other major city: Samarkand (395,000)
Highest point: In the south (4,643 m)
Official language: Uzbek
Main religion: Islam
Currency: Som (rouble also still in use)
Main exports: Cotton, chemicals, food, metals, minerals, machinery, textiles, gold
Government: Republic (transitional)
Per capita GNP: US $860

▼ *The dramatic skyline of the ancient town of Khiva. The view is dominated by soaring minarets and the dome of a mausoleum for the khans (Uzbek rulers) of the area.*

TAJIKISTAN

Tajikistan is a mountainous country, prone to earthquakes. In the Pamir Mountains snow makes the few roads impassable for more than six months a year. Yet in the fertile river valleys, where most people live, the summers are long and hot. The Tajiks are descended from the Persians, who first settled here thousands of years ago. The country has been invaded many times since and Islam was introduced by Arab conquerors in the AD600s. Today most Tajiks are Sunni Muslims. Minority groups include Uzbeks and Russians.

About two thirds of the population lives in rural areas, mostly along the rivers and in oases. Villagers grow mainly cotton, grain, vegetables, olives, figs and citrus fruits. Cattle breeding is important on the rich pasture lands. More and more rural people are moving to the cities to find jobs in Tajikistan's textile factories, steel works or other industries.

Tajikistan was controlled by the Soviet Union from the early 1920s. The Soviets brought many changes, such as building roads and schools, putting industry and agriculture under state control and discouraging religion. Opposition to their government reached a climax in the 1980s and Tajikistan gained independence in 1991. It then became a member of the Commonwealth of Independent States.

FACTS AND FIGURES
Area: 143,100 sq km
Population: 5,514,000
Capital: Dushanbe (592,000)
Other major city: Khudzhand (164,000)
Highest point: Communism Peak (7,495 m)
Official language: Tajik
Main religion: Islam
Currency: Rouble
Main exports: Cotton, food, metals, textiles, fruit, vegetables
Government: Republic
Per capita GNP: US $480

▲ *Snow stays on Moskva Peak in the rugged Pamir Mountains all year round. The nomads who wander this vast range call it the 'roof of the world'.*

▶ *At an open market in rural Tajikistan shoppers come to buy melons grown in the fierce summer heat. The men wear traditional embroidered skull caps.*

KYRGYZSTAN

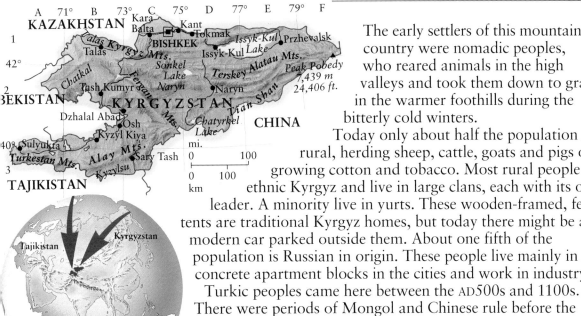

The early settlers of this mountainous country were nomadic peoples, who reared animals in the high valleys and took them down to graze in the warmer foothills during the bitterly cold winters.

Today only about half the population is rural, herding sheep, cattle, goats and pigs or growing cotton and tobacco. Most rural people are ethnic Kyrgyz and live in large clans, each with its own leader. A minority live in yurts. These wooden-framed, felt tents are traditional Kyrgyz homes, but today there might be a modern car parked outside them. About one fifth of the population is Russian in origin. These people live mainly in concrete apartment blocks in the cities and work in industry.

Turkic peoples came here between the AD500s and 1100s. There were periods of Mongol and Chinese rule before the Russians took over in the 1870s. Russia brought farm workers from other countries into the region, which left the nomads with fewer grazing grounds. In 1916 the Kyrgyz rebelled against Russian rule, but failed. Many thousands were killed, while thousands more fled to China. In 1922 the country came under Soviet rule. There were controls over the ways in which industry was run and land was used. The Soviets also banned the teaching of religion. In the late 1980s, however, they began to allow greater freedom and in 1991 Kyrgyzstan became an independent country.

FACTS AND FIGURES

Area: 198,500 sq km
Population: 4,528,000
Capital: Bishkek (642,000)
Other major city: Osh (239,000)
Highest point: Peak Pobedy (7,439 m)
Official language: Kyrgyz
Main religion: Islam
Currency: Som
Main exports: Food, machinery, manufactured products, wool, chemicals, metals
Government: Republic
Per capita GNP: US $810

▶ The Naryn, one of Kyrgyzstan's main rivers, runs through dramatic mountain scenery.

411

AFGHANISTAN

FACTS AND FIGURES
Area: 652,090 sq km
Population: 20,547,000
Capital: Kabul
(2,00,000)
Other major city:
Qandahar (179,000)
Highest point:
Nowshak (7,485 m)
Official languages:
Pashto, Dari
Main religion: Islam
Currency: Afghani
Main exports: Karakul
skins, raw cotton,
fruit and nuts,
natural gas, carpets
Government:
Single-party republic
Per capita GNP:
Est. under US $700

Afghanistan is a rugged country with many mountains. Its climate ranges from extreme heat to biting cold as the land rises from scorching deserts to towering, snow-capped peaks. A narrow corridor through the mountains, the Khyber Pass, links the country with Pakistan.

About 20 different ethnic groups live in Afghanistan, each with its own language and traditions. Some Afghans are semi-nomadic. In summer they roam the grasslands beneath the mountain peaks with their herds and sleep in tents made of felted goat hair. In winter they settle down to farm in the fertile valleys, where most people live. Only about ten percent of the population lives in towns and cities. These are mostly craftspeople who work at home. Afghanistan has relatively little industry.

Arabs swept into the region in the AD600s bringing their religion, Islam, with them. Over the following centuries Mongols, Iranians and native Afghans held power and Britain and Russia fought for control during the 1800s. By the 1970s Afghanistan was an independent country, but the Soviet Union had a great deal of power over the government because they supplied financial and military aid. Many of Afghanistan's Muslims believed that Soviet communist teachings went against their own traditions. A Muslim rebellion broke out and Soviet troops invaded in 1979, killing over one million Afghans. Ten years of civil war devastated the country and one quarter of the people fled the fighting. Many are still refugees in Pakistan and Iran. Soviet troops withdrew from Afghanistan in 1989, but conflict continued over who should govern the country and between different ethnic and religious groups.

▼ A Kyrgyz girl wears brightly coloured traditional dress and jewellery. The semi-nomadic Kyrgyz are one of the smallest of Afghanistan's ethnic groups. They live in the far northeast.

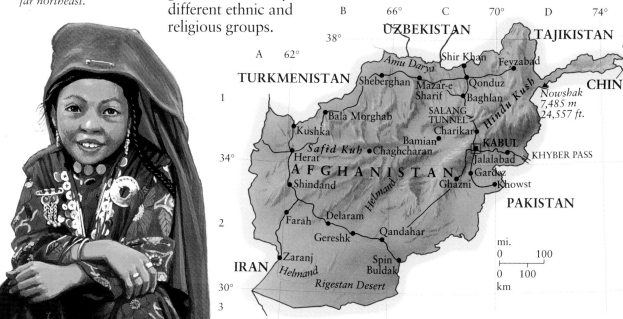

► *Shepherds with their flock of karakul sheep. Wool and sheepskins are some of Afghanistan's most important products. The curly fleece of young karakul lambs is highly prized for making coats and hats.*

► *A carpet seller spreads out his wares in an Afghan market. Brightly coloured woollen carpets like these, hand-woven in both traditional and modern designs, are now a major export.*

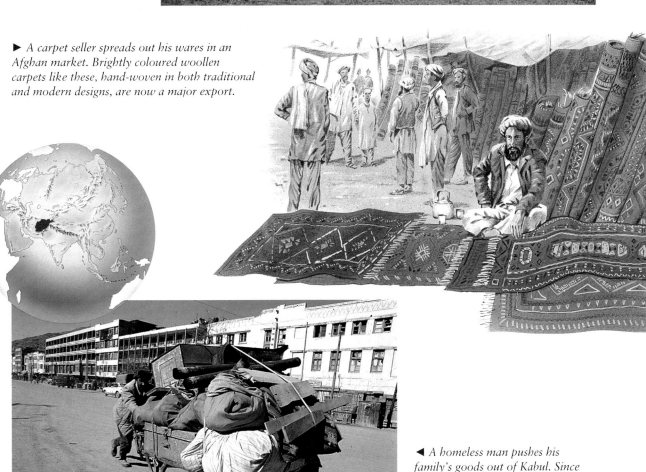

◄ *A homeless man pushes his family's goods out of Kabul. Since 1992 Afghanistan's capital has been the centre of a power struggle between rival groups within the country. Many thousands of refugees have fled the city because of destruction caused by the fighting.*

CYPRUS

The fertile island of Cyprus lies in the east of the Mediterranean Sea. Four fifths of its people are of Greek descent, while the rest are Turkish. Disagreements between the two groups have caused serious political problems. In 1974 a Turkish army invaded northern Cyprus and forced 200,000 Greek Cypriots to flee to the southern part of the island, where they still live today. The island remains divided although northern Cyprus is only recognized as an independent country by Turkey, where it is known as the Turkish Republic of Northern Cyprus.

Cyprus has played an important part in the history of the Mediterranean region and many peoples have contributed to its culture, including the Greeks, Egyptians, Romans, Byzantines, Venetians, French and Turks. Britain controlled the island from 1878 until its independence in 1960.

Today the rugged beauty of Cyprus, its historic sites, hilltop castles, sandy beaches and mild climate, have made tourism a major industry. Although many Cypriots now find work in the towns, agriculture is important. On the broad plain between the country's two mountain ranges farmers grow grapes, olives, potatoes and citrus fruits. There is also increasing industrial development, especially in the south.

▼ *Modern yachts and traditional fishing boats moor in Kyrenia harbour, northern Cyprus. Kyrenia has a long history as a port. In the town's Shipwreck Museum are the remains and cargo of a ship that sank just outside the harbour in about 300BC.*

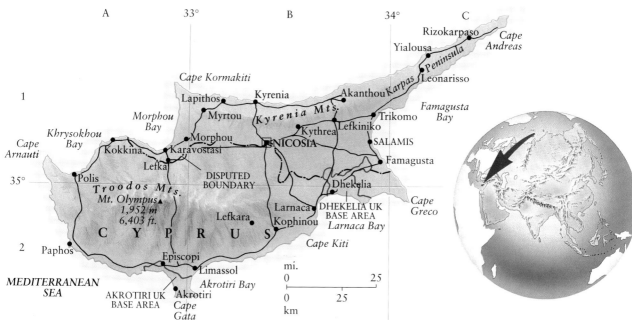

▶ *Villagers play* tavala *(the Cypriot name for backgammon). This dice game originated in Turkey and is popular throughout Turkish Cyprus, where men gather to play in local cafés.*

▼ *Village houses cluster round a church on a steep hillside in the Troodos Mountains. The mountains, protected by the state, are forested with dwarf oak, cypress and cedar and watered by swift-flowing streams. Copper has been mined in this part of Cyprus since Roman times.*

FACTS AND FIGURES
Area: 9,250 sq km
Population: 723,000
Capital: Nicosia (167,000)
Other major city: Limassol (130,000)
Highest point: Mt Olympus (1,952 m)
Official languages: Greek, Turkish
Main religions: Christianity, Islam
Currency: Cyprus pound
Main exports: Clothes, shoes, wine, potatoes, citrus fruit
Government: Constitutional republic
Per capita GNP: US $9,820

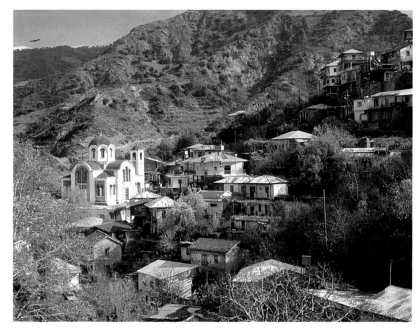

◀ *Folk dancing plays an important part in Cypriot life. People may dress in national costume to dance at religious feasts, weddings and other important occasions.*

TURKEY *Introduction*

Turkey has land in two continents, Asia and Europe. It commands an important waterway, the Bosporus, which joins the Black Sea to the Mediterranean. The land west of the Bosporus is European Turkey, while to the east lies the much larger Asian part of Turkey. Along the Black Sea coast are plains where farmers keep animals and cultivate fruit, nuts and tobacco. The most productive farmland is in the west. Wheat and maize are grown in the broad valleys and along the hot Mediterranean coast there are olive groves, orange trees and fields of cotton. Bears and wolves roam Turkey's mountains and forests. In farming areas sheep and goats graze around farmhouses made of stone or sun-dried brick.

A vast plateau extends across the centre of Turkey. Rimmed with mountains, this plateau has especially hot summers and cold winters. Turkey is also a land of lakes and rivers. Lake Van and Tuz Lake are large saltwater lakes and there are smaller freshwater lakes in the southwest. Many of the country's rivers dry up in the summer, but become fast-flowing torrents every spring, when they are used for hydroelectric power and irrigation.

About half the population lives in large towns. Some people work in coal and chromium mines, others in factories producing iron, steel, machinery and processed foods. People working in traditional cottage industries make carpets and pottery. Tourism is growing fast, particularly along the Mediterranean coast, where many holiday resorts are being built.

FACTS AND FIGURES
Area: 779,450 sq km
Population: 58,775,000
Capital: Ankara (3,023,000)
Other major cities: Istanbul (6,408,000), Izmir (2,666,000)
Highest point: Mt Ararat (5,123 m)
Official language: Turkish
Main religion: Islam
Currency: Turkish lira
Main exports: Textiles, iron, steel, tobacco, fruit, leather clothing, chemical products
Government: Multi-party republic
Per capita GNP: US $1,950

◀ *Hagia Sophia is a museum and one of Istanbul's most famous landmarks. It was built as a cathedral in the AD500s and was converted into a mosque in the 1400s.*

ENDANGERED WORLD
The loggerhead turtle breeds on beaches. Numbers are declining because of increasing tourism.

► In Cappadocia, a region west of Kayseri, some people live in buildings carved out of the cliffs. The yellow and pink volcanic rock has also been eroded by the weather into odd shapes.

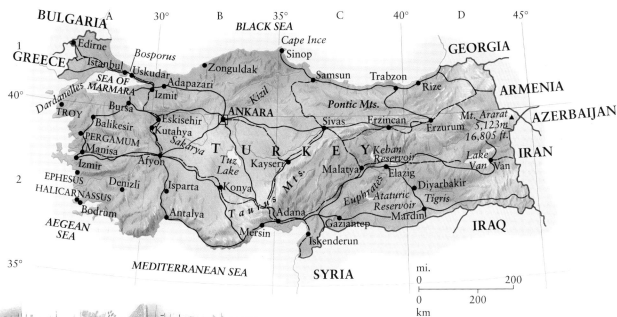

BULGARIA A 30° B 35° C 40° D 45°

1 GREECE

BLACK SEA

Cape Ince

GEORGIA

Edirne
Bosporus
Sinop
Istanbul
Uskudar Zonguldak Samsun Trabzon
ARMENIA
SEA OF Adapazari Rize
MARMARA Izmit
Kizil Pontic Mts. Mt. Ararat AZERBAIJAN
40° Dardanelles TROY Bursa Eskisehir ANKARA Sivas Erzincan Erzurum 5,123m 16,805 ft.
Balikesir Kutahya Lake IRAN
PERGAMUM Sakarya T U R K E Y Keban Van Van
Manisa Afyon Reservoir
Izmir Tuz Kayseri Malatya Elazig Diyarbakir
2 EPHESUS Denizli Lake Konya Euphrates Ataturic Tigris
HALICARNASSUS Isparta Taurus Mts. Adana Reservoir Mardin
Bodrum Antalya Gaziantep IRAQ
AEGEAN Mersin Iskenderun
SEA

35° MEDITERRANEAN SEA SYRIA

mi.
0 200

0 200
km

◄ Whirling dervishes are members of a Muslim sect who whirl and dance as part of their worship. Through the whirling, they enter a trance-like state in which they concentrate totally on spiritual matters.

TURKEY *People and History*

▲ *These Turkish women are spinning wool in the traditional way, using short sticks called spindles. By spinning the wool the fibres are twisted together to make a strong thread or yarn.*

Standing at the crossroads of two continents, Turkey has been a prized possession of some of the world's greatest empires. A people called the Hittites established themselves in the area around 1500BC and were followed by Persians and Greeks. By the AD400s this region was part of the mighty Byzantine empire, which was the eastern half of the Roman empire. The Byzantine capital was at Constantinople, now Istanbul. Seljuks, who were Muslims from central Asia, won control in the AD1000s and established Islam and the Turkish language. In the 1400s the Ottoman Turks made this region the centre of their empire and rapidly conquered the surrounding lands. The Ottoman empire, under its greatest sultan (ruler) Suleiman I, stretched from Hungary to Egypt and its navy controlled the Mediterranean Sea.

By 1600 the empire was in decline, although it did not finally break up until 1920. War against foreign powers in the early 1920s brought independence and Turkey became a republic in 1923. A military leader, Mustafa Kemal, became president and set out to make Turkey a modern, secular (non-religious) state. Kemal's reforms gained him the name Atatürk (Father of the Turks). He abolished Muslim schools and the Islamic legal system. Kemal also gave women the vote. Today Kemal's picture hangs in public buildings everywhere and his face is on all the banknotes.

SPEAK TURKISH

Hello – Merhaba
(*mer - hah - ba*)

Goodbye – Hoşça kalm
(*hosh - ja kal*)

Please – Lütfen (*lewt - fen*)

Thank you – Teşekkür ederim
(*tesh - e - kewr ed - e - rim*)

Yes – Evet (*eh - vet*)

No – Hayir (*hie - yerh*)

◄ Inside the magnificent Blue Mosque in Istanbul worshippers kneel to pray. They are facing Mecca, the holiest shrine in Islam. Although Turkey has no official state religion, most Turks are Muslims.

▼ This portrait of the Emperor Justinian is made of mosaic (coloured glass cubes set in plaster). Justinian ruled the Byzantine empire during the AD500s. He was famed for fair laws and for making the empire a centre of arts and learning.

◄ The Celsus Library, thought to date from AD110, is one of many fascinating ruins in the ancient city of Ephesus, founded by the Greeks. In AD262 the Goths destroyed much of Ephesus and it began a long decline.

419

SYRIA

Many thousands of years ago a Middle Eastern people called the Semites created a string of city states across what is now Syria. The ancient fortresses and mosques seen everywhere show that this is a country rich in history. Several of its cities are among the oldest in the world and the very first alphabet was developed here around 1500BC.

Ancient civilizations including the Persians, Romans and Ottoman Turks have all ruled this area. Muslim Arabs first settled during the AD600s, establishing Islam and the Arabic language. Today most people are Muslim Arabs. In this century first Turkey and then France took control. Since independence in 1946 Syria has been one of the leaders of Arab opposition to its Jewish neighbour Israel. Part of Syria, called the Golan Heights, has been occupied by Israel since 1967. Syria has also sent troops into Lebanon, where its army tried and failed to prevent civil war.

Syria is rapidly becoming more industrial. Many people are moving to the towns and cities from rural areas in search of jobs in the developing textile and chemical industries. About half the population still lives in farming villages along the coast, in the fertile river valleys and on the grassy western plains. These places have probably been cultivated since about 4000BC. A variety of other landscapes are found in this country, from arid deserts to snow-tipped mountains and pine and oak forests.

FACTS AND FIGURES
Area: 185,180 sq km
Population: 13,393,000
Capital: Damascus (1,497,000)
Other major cities: Aleppo (1,494,000), Homs (537,000), Latakia (293,000)
Highest point: Mt Hermon (2,814 m)
Official language: Arabic
Main religion: Islam
Currency: Syrian pound
Main exports: Petroleum and petroleum products, cotton, natural phosphate, fruit and vegetables
Government: Multi-party republic
Per capita GNP: Est. US $700-3,000

◀ These Syrian girls are wearing military cadet uniform. All Syrians between the ages of 15 and 18 have military training at school. Adult males over 18 years of age have to go on to do a further 30 months of military training when they leave school.

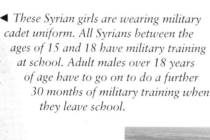

▼ Much of the city of Damascus now looks modern, but this is thought to be the oldest city in the world. Some ancient parts still exist, with narrow streets and markets.

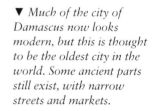

HUMMUS

Hummus is a spread made from crushed, shelled chickpeas. The spread is often mixed with tahini, a toasted sesame seed paste. Flavoured with garlic, lemon juice and salt, hummus with tahini has a delicious nutty taste. Syrians eat it with flat bread and olives.

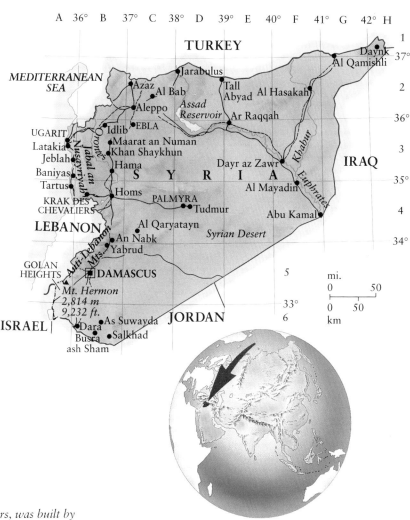

▼ This castle, called Krak des Chevaliers, was built by the Crusaders in the early 1200s. The Crusades were a series of wars fought during the early Middle Ages. The Christian Crusaders from Europe were trying to recapture the Holy Land (Palestine) from the Muslim Arabs.

421

LEBANON

A 36° B

MEDITERRANEAN SEA

Kebir
Halba

Tripoli

Al Hirmil

1

Qurnat as Sawda
▲ *3,083 m*
10,115 ft.

Al Batrun   Bsharri

L E B A N O N

Baalbek   *Anti-Lebanon Mts.*

34°   Juniyah

BEIRUT

Zahlah   Riyaq

Alayh   *Lebanon Mountains*

SYRIA

Sidon   Jazzin   Rashayya   *Litani*   *Bekaa Valley*

2

Marj Uyun   *Hasbani*

Tyre

Bint Jubayl   mi.
0   20

33°   0   20
ISRAEL   km

Lebanon is dominated by two mountain ranges, which run from north to south. The fertile farmlands of the Bekaa Valley lie sandwiched between them. Around 2500BC the seafaring Phoenicians became the first people to establish a civilization in this part of the world. Many centuries on, in the 1920s, the French were in control. Total independence from France came in 1946 and today most of the people are Arabs who have settled in the country's towns and cities. One quarter of the population lives in or around the capital. Some of the Arab population are Palestinians who believe that lands owned by Israel are rightfully theirs. The Palestine Liberation Organization (PLO) has been in conflict with Israel for many years and between 1969 and 1991 used Lebanon as a base for attacks on Israel. The country's Muslims and Christians have also had long-standing political differences which, combined with the Palestine-Israel dispute, led to the outbreak of civil war in 1975. The PLO supported the Muslims in this war. Troops from both Syria and Israel became involved and fighting continued until 1991. Some Israeli troops remained in the south and Syrian troops stayed in the Bekaa Valley to protect Muslim interests.

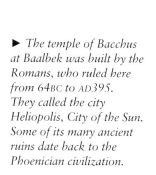

► *The temple of Bacchus at Baalbek was built by the Romans, who ruled here from 64BC to AD395. They called the city Heliopolis, City of the Sun. Some of its many ancient ruins date back to the Phoenician civilization.*

◀ A United Nations water truck heads into war-damaged Beirut in 1993. The United Nations sent a peacekeeping force to Lebanon in 1978, but fighting and terrorist bombings drove them out in 1984. The conflict ended in 1991 and much of Beirut was quickly rebuilt. Today the city is promoted as a tourist destination.

◀ This glass perfume bottle was made by the Phoenicians, a people who lived here from around 2500BC. The Phoenicians were great traders and explorers. They were also famous for inventing glass blowing and a purple dye made from shellfish.

FACTS AND FIGURES

Area: 10,450 sq km	**Main religions:**
Population: 2,901,000	Islam,
Capital: Beirut	Christianity
(1,500,000)	**Currency:**
Other major cities:	Lebanese pound
Tripoli (160,000),	**Main exports:** Clothes,
Zahlah (45,000)	jewellery, fruit
Highest point:	**Government:**
Qurnat as Sawda	Multi-party republic
(3,083 m)	**Per capita GNP:**
Official language: Arabic	Est. US $700-3,000

▶ These splendid cedars are found to the north of Baalbek. Cedars once covered the mountains of Lebanon, but were cut down for timber. Today these ancient trees are protected. Lebanese nurseries are also growing millions of seedlings to replant the forests.

ISRAEL *Introduction*

Israel was founded in 1948 as a home for Jews from all over the world. During the following years, many immigrants have brought all kinds of skills to the country. New industries, technologies and farming techniques have been developed and the standard of living is high. Along the coast is a fertile plain. This is the country's most important farming and industrial region. Hills run down the centre of Israel from north to south. Here, there are farms in the valleys, but much of the land is used for grazing. Some northern and eastern parts of Israel were once infertile, as was the arid Negev Desert. Since the 1950s, however, water has been pumped from the Sea of Galilee to irrigate the land. Now olives grow in dry northern parts, while potatoes and tomatoes flourish in the Negev.

Israel's capital, Jerusalem, is a holy city for Jews, Christians and Muslims. For Christians it is the site of Christ's burial place. For Jews it has the Western Wall, all that remains of the holy Temple of biblical times. Its main Muslim shrine is the Dome of the Rock, believed to be the place from which Muhammad rose to heaven.

Since Israel was created in 1948, there have been years of bitter fighting between the Jews and their Arab neighbours. The Arabs believe that Israel is occupying lands that should belong to their people. In 1994 peace agreements between Israel, the Palestine Liberation Organization and Jordan brought hopes that co-operation would replace warfare.

◀ *The Dead Sea is the world's lowest body of water. It is so salty that swimmers can float with ease. Few plants and no fish live there. The hot sun evaporates the water, leaving strange salt formations behind.*

SPEAK HEBREW

Hello – שלום
(sha - lom)

Goodbye – שלום
(sha - lom)

Please – בבקשה
(bee - vak - a - shah)

Thank you – תודה
(toh - dah)

▲ *Wadi Farah lies between Nabulus and the river Jordan. This area was arid and infertile until it was irrigated by the National Water Carrier. This is a system of canals, pipelines and tunnels that pumps water from the Sea of Galilee and the river Jordan. Fruit trees and vegetables can now be grown in the desert.*

FACTS AND FIGURES

Area: 21,950 sq km
Population: 5,256,000
Capital: Jerusalem (557,000)
Other major cities:
Tel Aviv (357,000),
Haifa (250,000),
Petah Tiqwa (151,000),
Bat Yam (146,000)
Highest point:
Mt Meron (1,208 m)
Official languages:
Hebrew, Arabic

Main religions:
Judaism, Islam,
Christianity
Currency: Shekel
Main exports:
Fruit, vegetables,
oil products, chemical
products, diamonds,
machinery, fertilizers
Government:
Multi-party republic
Per capita GNP:
US $13,230

FELAFEL

Felafel are little round patties made of chickpeas. They are deep-fried to a crisp golden brown. Israelis often eat them on their own as a snack. Alternatively they can form part of a meal, stuffed into pitta bread with a crunchy salad of cucumber, lettuce, tomato and hot chilli pepper. Felafel are sold from barrows on many busy Israeli streets.

ISRAEL *People and History*

▲ *A Jewish man blows on a shofar, a ram's horn fitted with a reed. The shofar is one of the world's oldest musical instruments and is blown on Jewish High Holy days. The woven prayer shawl is called a tallith.*

Israel is part of a historic land called Palestine. Today the word Palestine refers to most of Israel, although ancient Palestine extended farther east. Palestine is also known as the Holy Land, where both the Jewish and Christian faiths began. By about 1000BC the Hebrew people (also called Israelites) had founded the kingdom of Israel here. Israel grew powerful under its great kings, David and Solomon, but after Solomon's death in 922BC it divided. The northern part was called Israel and the southern part Judah. Judah is the origin of the name Jew, by which the Hebrews came to be known. In about 500BC Judah was captured by the Babylonians and many Jews were exiled. Although some returned later, this was the start of the Diaspora – the scattering of Jews from their homeland to settle all over Europe and Asia. The process continued after the Roman conquest of 63BC. During the AD600s Palestine was conquered by the Muslim Arabs. In 1516 it became part of the Ottoman empire. By this time many people in Palestine were Muslim Arabs, although a Jewish community remained.

In the late 1800s Jews abroad started Zionism, a movement to establish a Jewish state in Palestine. Jews began to immigrate to Palestine, causing tensions with Palestinian Arabs. In 1948 the Jewish state of Israel declared itself independent and was immediately attacked by its Arab neighbours. A ceasefire in 1949 was followed by more Arab-Israeli wars. In the 1960s Israel occupied Arab land on the Gaza Strip, the West Bank, the Golan Heights and the Sinai Peninsula. Egypt and Israel signed an agreement in the 1970s and by 1994 Jews and Arabs were working together to establish peace.

◀ *Arab students study at a Palestinian school in the Gaza Strip. This was Israeli-occupied territory from 1967 to 1993, when the Palestinians were given partial control of the area.*

► *The Western Wall is in the foreground of this view of Jerusalem. This is the western wall of the holy Temple, which was used in biblical times. Today many Jews go on a pilgrimage to pray there. Behind the wall is the Dome of the Rock, sacred to Muslims.*

▲ *Workers pick oranges on a kibbutz, a collective farm where work and profits are shared. The famous Jaffa oranges are named after Tel Aviv's old town, which is known as Jaffa. They are grown on the fertile Plain of Sharon.*

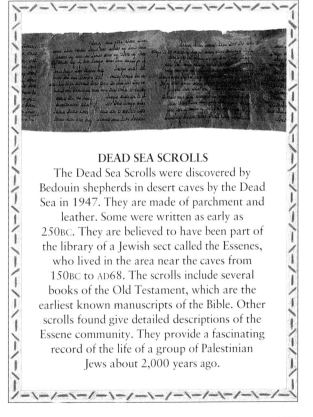

DEAD SEA SCROLLS

The Dead Sea Scrolls were discovered by Bedouin shepherds in desert caves by the Dead Sea in 1947. They are made of parchment and leather. Some were written as early as 250BC. They are believed to have been part of the library of a Jewish sect called the Essenes, who lived in the area near the caves from 150BC to AD68. The scrolls include several books of the Old Testament, which are the earliest known manuscripts of the Bible. Other scrolls found give detailed descriptions of the Essene community. They provide a fascinating record of the life of a group of Palestinian Jews about 2,000 years ago.

JORDAN

Jordan is an Arab nation in the heart of the Middle East. It is a hot, dry country of deserts, mountains, deep valleys and scrubby plains. Jordan's long history has left it with many spectacular monuments, the remains of ancient cities built by the peoples who once ruled here, such as the Nabateans, Greeks, Romans and Ottoman Turks.

After a brief period of British control, from 1921 to 1946, Jordan gained complete independence. The country then became involved in the Palestinian conflict. When the new state of Israel was set up in Palestine in 1948, Jordan and Israel's other Arab neighbours attacked it. Jordan took control of some of the former Palestinian territory including the West Bank. During the Six-Day War of 1967 Jordan lost the West Bank to Israel and refugees poured into Jordan. Many of them joined the Palestine Liberation Organization (PLO), which organized terrorist attacks on Israel from bases in Jordan and other Arab countries. Conflict between the PLO and the Jordanian government of King Hussein led to a civil war in 1970. King Hussein's government was defeated within a month, but fighting continued between various groups. In 1994 Jordan signed a peace treaty with Israel.

The majority of the population in this Muslim country are Jordanian Arabs. There are also a large number of Palestinians, mostly refugees from the Arab-Israeli wars. Around ten percent still live in refugee camps, but most Jordanians live in towns and cities. Many work for the government or in service industries such as finance, trade and tourism. Much of the land is infertile, so there is little large-scale agriculture. However, vegetables and citrus fruits are grown in the Jordan river valley.

▲ The buildings of ancient Petra have been carved out of solid rock. This beautiful city was built in about 400BC as the capital of the Nabateans, an Arab people. It is sometimes called the 'rose-red city' because of the colour of the rock from which it is built.

FACTS AND FIGURES

Area: 91,880 sq km
Population: 4,440,000
Capital: Amman (1,272,000)
Other major city: Az Zarqa (605,000)
Highest point: Jabal Ramm (1,754 m)
Official language: Arabic

Main religion: Islam
Currency: Jordan dinar
Main exports: Phosphate, potash, fertilizers, fruit and vegetables
Government: Constitutional monarchy
Per capita GNP: US $1,120

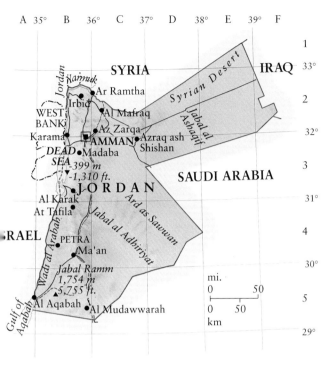

A 35°   B   36°   C   37°   D   38°   E   39°   F

SYRIA

IRAQ

Jordan

Yarmuk

Ar Ramtha

Irbid

Al Mafraq

WEST BANK

Az Zarqa

Karama

AMMAN

Azraq ash Shishan

DEAD SEA

Madaba

Jabal al Ashaqif

-399 m

-1,310 ft.

JORDAN

SAUDI ARABIA

Al Karak

At Tafila

Jabal al Adhiriyat

Ard as Sauwan

ISRAEL

PETRA

Wadi al Arabah

Ma'an

Jabal Ramm
1,754 m
5,755 ft.

Gulf of Aqabah

Al Aqabah

Al Mudawwarah

mi.
0   50

0   50
km

▼ These men are members of the Jordanian army's famous Desert Patrol. The Desert Patrol was set up in 1931 to police the border with Saudi Arabia. Its members' distinctive uniform was designed for practical wear in the extreme temperatures of the desert.

◀ A boy sells oranges outside the Abu Darwish mosque in Amman as people go in to pray. Arab conquerors brought Islam to Jordan in the AD600s. Since then it has been on an important pilgrimage route to the Muslim holy city of Mecca in Saudi Arabia.

IRAQ *Introduction*

Iraq is an Arab state at the top of the Persian Gulf. In the west and southwest are wide expanses of desert. The only people who live there are Bedouins, moving with their camels between oases fringed with date-palms. In the northeast rugged mountains form the border with Iran and Turkey. This region also provides scrubby pasture for goats and sheep.

The foothills of these mountains are home to many Kurds, semi-nomadic people who make up about 20 percent of Iraq's population. At the heart of the country lies the capital Baghdad, which is one of the largest cities in the Middle East.

South of Baghdad a green and fertile plain opens up between the Tigris and Euphrates rivers. It is part of an area once called Mesopotamia, meaning 'the land between the rivers'. The world's earliest known civilization, ancient Sumer, developed there about 3500BC. Today most of Iraq's population lives on the plain, which has become the centre of the country's agriculture and industry. There are oil and sugar refineries, tanneries and factories producing cotton and cement. In the southeast are wetlands, a haven for kingfishers and storks, wild boar and ibis. For at least five thousand years this wetland region has been home to a people called the Marsh Arabs, who fish and farm using complicated systems of irrigation and drainage.

Iraq's economy is built on oil reserves, which are especially vast in the south. In 1990 Iraq invaded Kuwait. This led to the Gulf War, which Iraq lost. The United Nations banned Iraq from selling oil until it had paid Kuwait for the devastation caused by the war. This was a severe blow to the Iraqi economy, already badly damaged by eight years of war with Iran in the 1980s.

FACTS AND FIGURES
Area: 438,320 sq km
Population: 19,918,000
Capital: Baghdad (3,850,000)
Other major cities:
Al Basrah (617,000), Mosul (571,000), Kirkuk (570,000), Irbil (334,000)
Highest point:
In the Zagros Mountains (3,608 m)
Official language: Arabic
Main religion: Islam
Currency: Iraqi dinar
Main exports:
Petroleum, wool, dates
Government:
Single-party republic
Per capita GNP:
Est. US $700-3,000

◄ *The Ramadan mosque stands in an area of Baghdad that was swiftly rebuilt soon after the destruction of the 1991 Gulf War. Although reconstruction is a major industry in Iraq, many homes are still without water or drainage.*

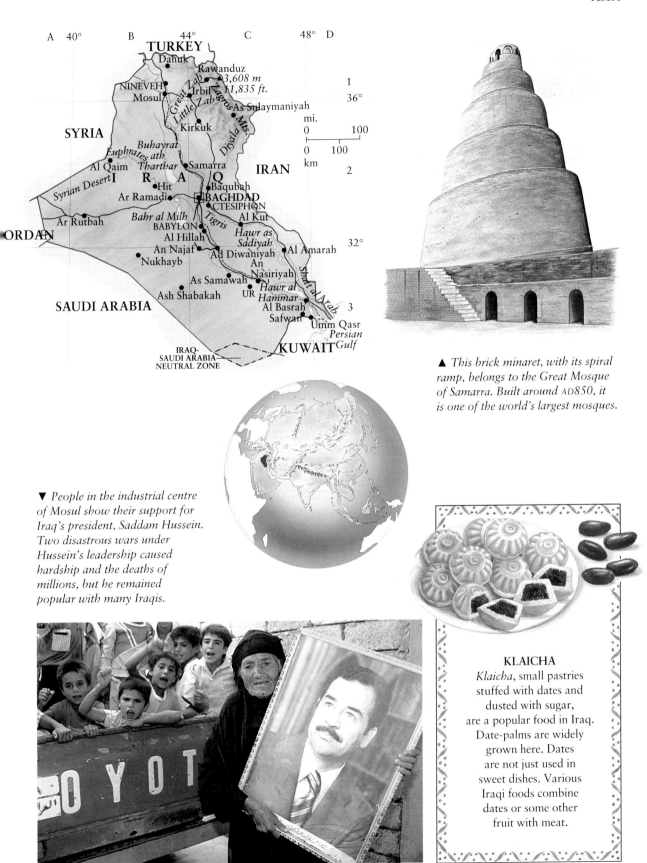

TURKEY

Dahuk
Rawanduz
NINEVEH
Mosul
3,608 m
Irbil
11,835 ft.
As Sulaymaniyah

SYRIA

Great Zab
Little Zab
Zagros Mts.
Kirkuk
Diyala

Buhayrat
ath
Tharthar
Euphrates
Samarra
Al Qaim

IRAN

Syrian Desert
I R A Q
Hit
Baqubah
Ar Ramadi
BAGHDAD
CTESIPHON

ORDAN

Ar Rutbah
Bahr al Milh
Al Kut
BABYLON
Tigris
Al Hillah
Hawr as
Sadiyah
An Najaf
Al Amarah
Nukhayb
Ad Diwaniyah
An
Nasiriyah
As Samawah
Shatt al Arab
UR
Ash Shabakah
Hawr al
Hammar
Al Basrah
Safwan

SAUDI ARABIA

Umm Qasr
Persian
Gulf
IRAQ-
SAUDI ARABIA
NEUTRAL ZONE
KUWAIT

A 40° B 44° C 48° D
1
36°
mi.
0   100
0   100
km
2
32°
3

▲ *This brick minaret, with its spiral ramp, belongs to the Great Mosque of Samarra. Built around* AD850, *it is one of the world's largest mosques.*

▼ *People in the industrial centre of Mosul show their support for Iraq's president, Saddam Hussein. Two disastrous wars under Hussein's leadership caused hardship and the deaths of millions, but he remained popular with many Iraqis.*

KLAICHA

Klaicha, small pastries stuffed with dates and dusted with sugar, are a popular food in Iraq. Date-palms are widely grown here. Dates are not just used in sweet dishes. Various Iraqi foods combine dates or some other fruit with meat.

431

IRAQ *People and History*

By about 3000BC the Sumerian people were establishing a great civilization in this region. It was the Sumerians who invented the art of writing, using wedge-shaped symbols scratched onto wet clay tablets. Archaeologists have dug up many Sumerian tablets and the earliest inscriptions found so far were discovered in southeastern Iraq. The Sumerian civilization declined towards 2000BC. Then other ancient civilizations – Assyria and Babylonia – grew up in Mesopotamia. From about 500BC its conquerors included the Persians, Greeks and Arabs. The Arabs brought the Islamic religion and made Baghdad the capital of their empire.

The Ottoman Turks were a force in the area for many centuries, after invading Mesopotamia in 1534. By the start of this century their glory had waned. Britain then took some control and Iraq did not gain independence until 1932. After 1950 the country's oil industry brought prosperity. However, Iraq was shattered by war under Saddam Hussein, who became president in 1979. First he invaded Iran, starting a war that lasted from 1980 until 1988. Hussein then invaded Kuwait, sparking the Gulf War of 1991.

The majority of Iraqis live in towns and cities, working in business, government, factories or the oilfields. Both the Kurdish people and the Marsh Arabs have been persecuted by the Iraqi government and many have fled the country. The Kurds have long been fighting for self-rule and the Marsh Arabs are Shiite Muslims who do not support Saddam Hussein, a Sunni Muslim. Life is difficult for most other Iraqis because war has destroyed homes and jobs. Also sanctions (international trade restrictions) have caused shortages of food and medicine.

▲ *This gold pendant was found in a grave at Ur, once the capital of the Sumerian civilization. It is thought that when royalty died their servants were killed and buried alongside them. Both royalty and servants were buried still wearing their jewellery.*

◀ *Craftsmen work on brass trays, beating out their shape and design with hammers. Fine metalwork has been a tradition in Iraq for many thousands of years. Pitchers, pots and trays are among the country's specialities.*

◄ The houses of the Marsh Arabs are built from reeds. They are often constructed on floating platforms woven from the tips of reeds still growing up out of the swamp. The people travel about the swamp by canoe. The Marsh Arabs' lifestyle is threatened by drainage projects that are taking water from the swamps, causing them to dry up.

► The palace at Ctesiphon dates from the AD500s. The arch is the remains of an enormous hall with a vaulted ceiling (a ceiling held up by curved ribs). Ctesiphon was the capital city of the Parthian empire. It was also occupied by the Greeks and Romans, but was abandoned when the Arabs came and founded nearby Baghdad around AD765.

◄ Kurdish refugees take a rest on their journey to Iran. In 1991 the Kurds rebelled against Saddam Hussein, demanding self-rule. Hussein replied with a massacre. Thousands were killed or died of starvation or disease. More than two million fled into the mountains bordering Iran and Turkey.

IRAN *Introduction*

Iran is a country of mountains, deserts and fertile valleys. About 70 percent of the land is sparsely populated. The centre of Iran, a vast plateau, is an empty desert of salt, sand and gravel. To the north the Elburz Mountains slope down to the land-locked Caspian Sea. In these warm waters sturgeon are fished for their eggs, known as caviar. The coastal plain and valleys are green and productive. Farmers living in scattered villages grow tobacco, cotton and tea, while nomads travel with herds of donkeys and sleep in round tents of black felt, called yurts.

In the southeast the Khuzestan Plain is an important agricultural area. It is also the site of Iran's major oilfields. Iran is one of the world's leading oil producers, although revolution and war have caused its output to drop since 1979. Oil is also drilled in the Iranian waters of the Persian Gulf. There is a big oil terminal just off the coast at Kharg Island.

In rural areas many Iranian men wear the traditional long coat and black, baggy trousers. In the towns and cities, however, men usually wear Western dress. Most city women are cloaked in a black robe called a chadar. Some Islamic religious teachings tell women to cover themselves like this. About half the population of Iran lives in cities, often working in manufacturing or service industries. In the traditional parts of towns and cities Iranians shop in the bazaar, a market with tiny passageways under domed brick roofs. The stalls sell crafts such as jewellery, pottery, metalware and the rugs for which the country is famous.

▼ *The Madrasa-i Chahar Bagh is in Isfahan. It was built in the 1700s as a college for religious studies. Isfahan has some of the most beautiful examples of Islamic architecture in Iran.*

◀ *The city of Teheran is at the foot of the Elburz Mountains. It is Iran's largest city and its capital. There are modern schools, hospitals, offices and apartment blocks alongside traditional homes built of mud bricks. Teheran has been the capital of Iran since the late 1700s.*

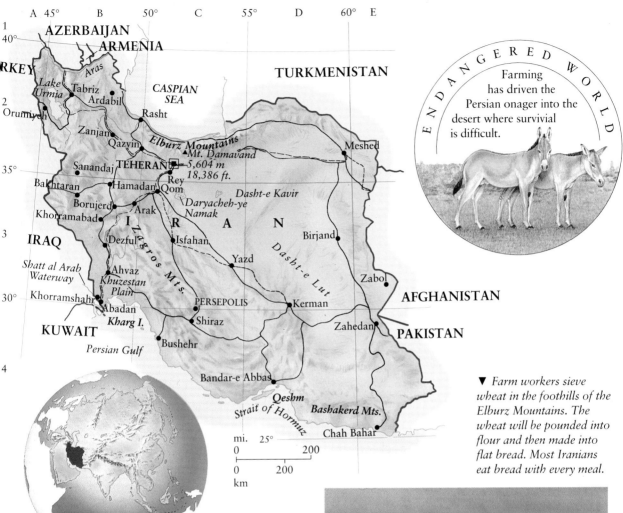

A 45° B 50° C 55° D 60° E

AZERBAIJAN
ARMENIA
RKEY
Aras
Lake Urmia Tabriz
Ardabil
Orumiyeh
CASPIAN SEA
Zanjan
Rasht
Qazvin
Elburz Mountains
▲ *Mt. Damavand*
5,604 m
18,386 ft.
Sanandaj **TEHERAN**
Rey
Bakhtaran Hamadan Qom
Borujerd Arak
Khorramabad *Daryacheh-ye Namak*
Dasht-e Kavir
I R A N
Dezful Isfahan
Birjand
Ahvaz Yazd
Khuzestan Plain
Shatt al Arab Waterway
Dasht-e Lut
Zabol
Khorramshahr
Abadan PERSEPOLIS Kerman
Kharg I. Shiraz
Zahedan **PAKISTAN**
KUWAIT
Persian Gulf Bushehr
Bandar-e Abbas
Qeshm
Strait of Hormuz *Bashakerd Mts.*
Chah Bahar

TURKMENISTAN
Meshed

IRAQ

AFGHANISTAN

mi. 25°
0   200
0   200
km

E N D A N G E R E D W O R L D
Farming has driven the Persian onager into the desert where survivial is difficult.

▼ *Farm workers sieve wheat in the foothills of the Elburz Mountains. The wheat will be pounded into flour and then made into flat bread. Most Iranians eat bread with every meal.*

FACTS AND FIGURES

Area: 1,648,000 sq km
Population: 63,180,000
Capital: Teheran (6,043,000)
Other major cities: Meshed (1,464,000), Isfahan (987,000), Tabriz (972,000)
Highest point: Mt Damavand (5,604 m)
Official language: Farsi (Persian)
Main religion: Islam

Currency: Rial
Main exports: Petroleum, carpets, fruit, cotton, textiles, metalwork
Government: Islamic republic
Per capita GNP: US $2,190

435

IRAN *People and History*

▼ *Iran's religious leader, Ayatollah Khamenei, makes a speech in 1994. The picture is of his predecessor, Ayatollah Khomeini, who died in 1989. The country's religious leader also holds enormous political power.*

Iran used to be called Persia. Its first civilized society probably established itself over five thousand years ago. Most Iranians are descendants of migrants from central Asia, who first settled the area around 1500BC. Arab conquerors brought Islam to Persia about AD600 and the arts and sciences flourished for several centuries. The Mongols, led by Genghis Khan, invaded in 1220. By the early 1500s they had been replaced by the dynasty of the Safavids. During the 1800s the British and Russian empires struggled over control of Iranian territory.

Reza Pahlavi, an officer in the Iranian cavalry, became shah (king) in 1925. He was succeeded by his son, Mohammed Reza Pahlavi. Large oilfields had been discovered in Iran in the early 1900s and both shahs used the profits from Iran's new oil industry to modernize the country. They made social and economic improvements, but ruled Iran as dictators.

The Muslim leader, Ayatollah Khomeini, led a revolution that overthrew the shah in 1979. He made Iran an Islamic republic, governed by strict religious law. Freedom of speech and other civil rights, especially women's rights, were taken away. Modernization was stopped and the economy suffered. In 1980 war broke out with Iraq. It was started by a dispute over the Shatt al Arab Waterway, the important oil route that divides the two countries. The eight-year war killed thousands, destroyed factories and cut oil exports. A new government came to power in the early 1990s and set about finding solutions to the economic problems caused by the war.

▶ *Iranian women weave a rug in the traditional way. Made of wool or silk, the rugs are prized for their rich colours and intricate patterns. In some Iranian homes the rug serves as table, chair and bed.*

STUFFED QUINCES

These quinces are stuffed with minced meat and spiced with cinnamon. Apples are sometimes used instead of quinces. Fruit and meat are often eaten together in Iran. Mixing sweet and sour flavours started with the Persians.

SPEAK FARSI

Hello – سلام
(sa - lahm)

Goodbye – خدا حافظ
(kho - da ha - fez)

Please – خواهش میکنم
(kha - hesh mee - ko - nam)

Thank you – متشکرم
(moo - te - sha - ke - ram)

▼ *This Persian miniature painting shows King Bahram Gur killing two lions. The story is told in Farsi script at the top. The Persians were famous for their detailed and brilliantly coloured miniatures. They often illustrated scenes from traditional poems.*

◄ *The ruins of the great city of Persepolis are still a magnificent sight. The capital of King Darius I of Persia was built on a spectacular mountain site around 520BC. Its palaces and administrative buildings were decorated with splendid sculptures of people and animals, carved in limestone.*

KUWAIT

Kuwait is a small desert country at the top of the Persian Gulf. There are no lakes or rivers, so distilled seawater is the main source of fresh water. Kuwait has large oilfields and the vast profits made from exporting oil have turned it into one of the richest countries in the world.

Until the early 1700s the area that is now Kuwait was almost uninhabited. Then Arabs of the Anaza peoples settled in Kuwait Bay and built a port there. This became Kuwait City, which is now the country's capital. In 1899 the ruler of Kuwait appealed to Britain for protection against the Turks, who had tried to take control of the country. Britain was responsible for Kuwait's defence until it became fully independent in 1961. After 1946 Kuwait began to export oil on a large-scale and the once-poor country was transformed. Today it has free education and healthcare. There is no income tax and the government subsidizes food, transport and services. It is investing profits from oil in irrigation projects so that crops can be grown in some desert areas. The government is also trying to develop other industries to increase employment opportunities.

In 1990 Kuwait was invaded by Iraq. In 1991 Allied forces, including troops from the United Kingdom and the United States of America, drove out the Iraqis. The Iraqis retaliated with bombs, setting hundreds of oil wells on fire. Kuwait's economy was badly damaged and the land and sea polluted. However, after the war rebuilding of the damaged areas was rapid.

▲ *Spectacular water towers dominate the skyline of Kuwait City. The water towers are part of desalination plants that turn seawater into fresh water by removing the salt. Fresh water is scarce in Kuwait and these plants are its main source.*

◄ *These women were among the first female oil workers in Kuwait. Few Kuwaiti women were educated or had jobs outside the home before 1960. Now increasing numbers study at Kuwait University and work in business and industry.*

FACTS AND FIGURES
Area: 17,820 sq km
Population: 1,433,000
Capital: Kuwait City (32,000)
Other major city: As Salimiyah (117,000)
Highest point: In the west (283 m)
Official language: Arabic
Main religion: Islam
Currency: Kuwaiti dinar
Main exports: Petroleum
Government: Monarchy (emir is head of state)
Per capita GNP: Est. over US $9,000

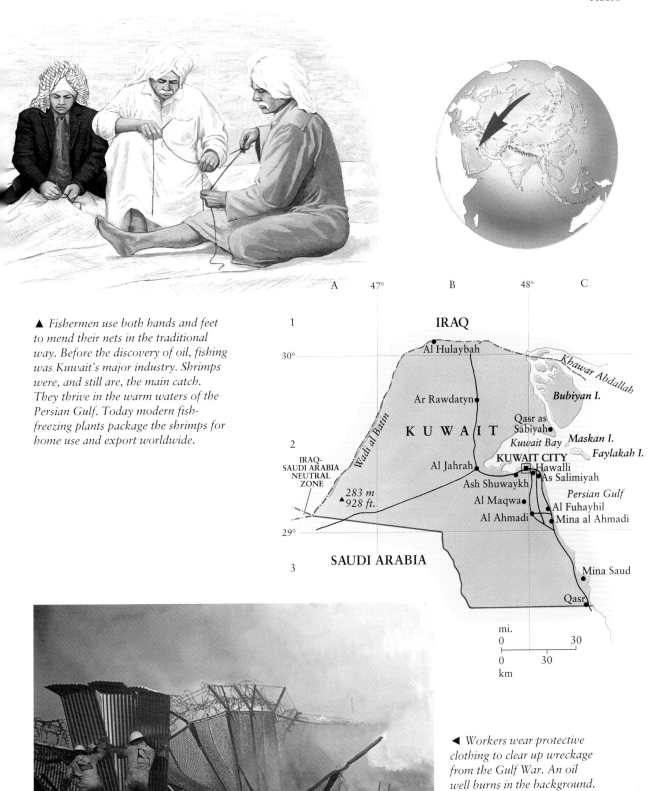

▲ Fishermen use both hands and feet to mend their nets in the traditional way. Before the discovery of oil, fishing was Kuwait's major industry. Shrimps were, and still are, the main catch. They thrive in the warm waters of the Persian Gulf. Today modern fish-freezing plants package the shrimps for home use and export worldwide.

◄ Workers wear protective clothing to clear up wreckage from the Gulf War. An oil well burns in the background. During the war the Iraqis set fire to many oil wells. Afterwards a multinational effort went into restoring Kuwait's environment.

439

SAUDI ARABIA *Introduction*

Saudi Arabia occupies most of the huge barren waste of the Arabian Peninsula. It has no permanent rivers or lakes, only wadis (valleys where rain collects, then drains away or dries out in the sun). This desert kingdom is enormously wealthy because it has the biggest oil deposits in the world. It is one of the world's leading producers of petroleum.

In the middle of Saudi Arabia is the Central Plateau. Here, under the fierce heat of the scorching sun, nomads may be found wandering in search of grass for their herds of goats, sheep and camels. To the south lies a huge desert called the Rub al Khali (Empty Quarter). There are no landmarks in this area to guide travellers because winds whip up terrific sandstorms that make the dunes change their shapes. To the north is more desert of rock, sand and gravel.

In the west, bordering the Red Sea, are low, rocky mountains. Their slopes are Saudi Arabia's most fertile area. Farmers grow wheat, melons and dates on small terraced fields. They also keep chickens outside their houses of stone or baked mud.

The oil industry is based in the eastern lowlands on the Persian Gulf. There, modern cities such as Dhahran have sprung up. Cars share roads with camels and apartment blocks tower above huts of mud. The Saudis are developing new industries and expanding agricultural production to keep the economy stable after oil resources run out.

FACTS AND FIGURES
Area: 2,200,000 sq km
Population: 16,472,000
Capital: Riyadh (1,500,000)
Other major cities: Jiddah (1,400,000), Mecca (618,000), Medina (500,000)
Highest point: Jabal Sawda (3,207 m)
Official language: Arabic
Main religion: Islam
Currency: Riyal
Main exports: Petroleum and petroleum products, wheat and dates
Government: Monarchy
Per capita GNP: US $7,940

PRAWN BALLS
Prawn balls are flavoured with the spices coriander and turmeric. They are eaten with a tamarind sauce, which is both bitter and sweet. Delicate, spicy foods like this have a cooling effect in the searing heat of Saudi Arabia. The prawn balls are served with rice, which is eaten at most Saudi meals.

▼ *The Saudi royal family enjoy a day out at the races in Riyadh. The Saud dynasty (ruling family) has reigned over much of the Arabian Peninsula since the late 1700s.*

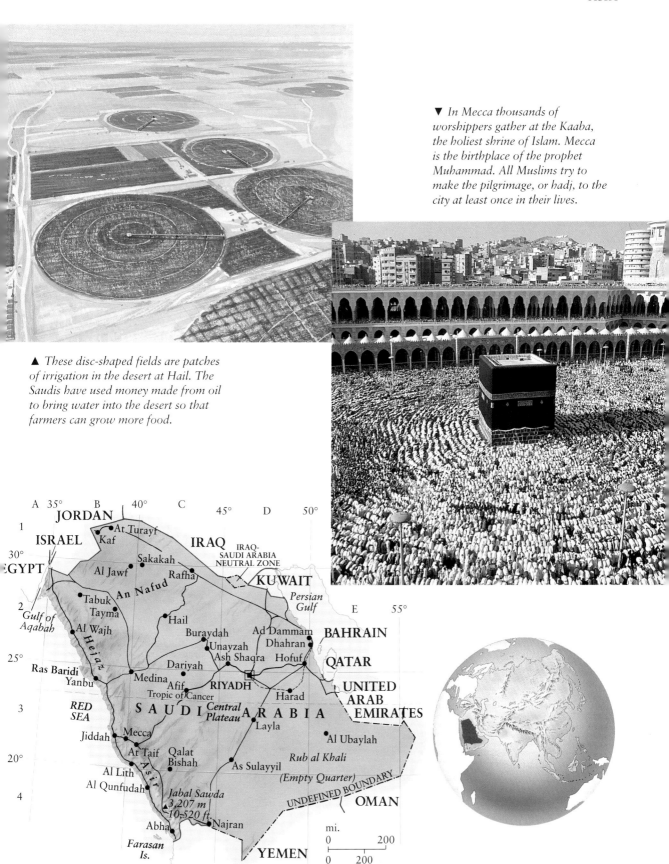

▼ In Mecca thousands of worshippers gather at the Kaaba, the holiest shrine of Islam. Mecca is the birthplace of the prophet Muhammad. All Muslims try to make the pilgrimage, or hadj, to the city at least once in their lives.

▲ These disc-shaped fields are patches of irrigation in the desert at Hail. The Saudis have used money made from oil to bring water into the desert so that farmers can grow more food.

441

SAUDI ARABIA *People and History*

Saudi Arabia is the home of Islam, the religion founded by Muhammad around AD600. Under Islamic law the king is also the imam (religious leader) and the prime minister. The royal family, including about five thousand princes, is the most important political group. The strict form of Islam practised by Saudis has a major influence on everyday life. Women, for example, have little freedom outside the home.

A large proportion of the population are descendants of traders who settled in the Arabian Peninsula more than two thousand years ago. There are also large numbers of Bedouin Arabs. Some Bedouins lead a traditional nomadic life that has changed little for centuries.

During the early 1800s the Saud family, rulers of a small area around Riyadh, expanded their territory by conquest to include most of what is now Saudi Arabia. Civil war and opposition from the Turks, who controlled large parts of the Arabian Peninsula from the 1500s, wiped out their gains. In the early 1900s the Turks' power faded and Saudi forces, led by Ibn Saud, recaptured the lost territory. By 1932 Saudi Arabia had become a kingdom with Ibn Saud as its first king.

From the 1940s oil wealth brought prosperity to Saudi Arabia and made it a leading power in the Middle East. The standard of living rose quickly with the development of modern healthcare, schools, housing and roads. Until the discovery of oil most Saudis lived in rural areas, but today three quarters of the population lives in cities. Many have come to Saudi Arabia from other countries in search of work.

▼ *This Bedouin family live in a tent made of animal skins. Many Bedouins still follow their traditional nomadic lives in the desert, but some have become farmers or work in the cities.*

▼ *These ruins are part of Dariyah, which was the capital city until the early 1800s. Dariyah was captured and destroyed by the Turks in 1819 and never rebuilt. Instead the capital was moved to nearby Riyadh.*

▲ *This municipal office building is in Jiddah, the second largest city in Saudi Arabia. It is built in traditional Islamic style with domed archways and latticed windows. Lattices (criss-cross strips of wood or metal) help to keep out the glare of the sun.*

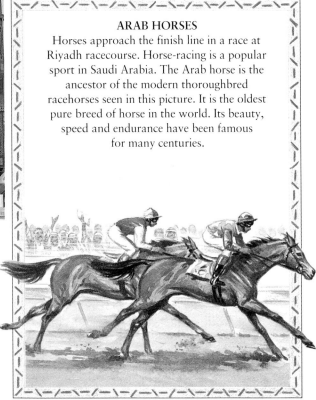

ARAB HORSES
Horses approach the finish line in a race at Riyadh racecourse. Horse-racing is a popular sport in Saudi Arabia. The Arab horse is the ancestor of the modern thoroughbred racehorses seen in this picture. It is the oldest pure breed of horse in the world. Its beauty, speed and endurance have been famous for many centuries.

◄ *Saudi men relax, sitting cross-legged on the carpet to drink tea and play dominoes or cards. Islamic traditions mean that there are never any women at gatherings like this. Both men and women are forbidden entertainments such as going to the theatre and drinking alcohol.*

443

YEMEN

In the northeast of Yemen is a baking, stony desert where years can pass without rain. On the mountains between the desert and the coastal plain monsoon rains come every winter. In the steep valleys farmers grow coffee, cotton, fruit and vegetables on terraced fields. Other Yemenis make their living by fishing in the sea, while many are craftspeople whose work fills colourful bazaars.

Since oil was discovered in the 1980s it has become vital to the economy. The construction industry is also very important. However, there are not enough jobs and many Yemenis work in other countries, mainly Saudi Arabia.

Nomadic herders have lived in this region for thousands of years. From 1500BC the area prospered as camel caravans moved across it, trading between Africa and India in pearls and spices. Islam came to Yemen in the AD600s. By 1517 it had joined the Turkish empire and in northern Yemen Turkish rule lasted until 1924. Southern Yemen came under British control in 1839, only gaining independence in 1967. The south was reunited with the north as the Republic of Yemen in 1990, but civil war broke out between the two in 1994.

▲ Sana is one of the most beautiful Arabian cities. Inside its ancient walls are mosques, palaces and bazaars of white stone and mud bricks.

◄ Curved daggers called djambias are carried by most Yemeni men. The daggers have ornately carved handles made of ivory or rhinoceros horn.

FACTS AND FIGURES
Area: 531,000 sq km
Population: 12,302,000
Capital: Sana (500,000)
Other major city: Aden (418,000)
Highest point: Mt Hadur Shuayb (3,760 m)
Official language: Arabic
Main religion: Islam
Currencies: Yemeni dinar, riyal
Main exports: Petroleum products, cotton, fish
Government: Republic
Per capita GNP: Est. under US $700

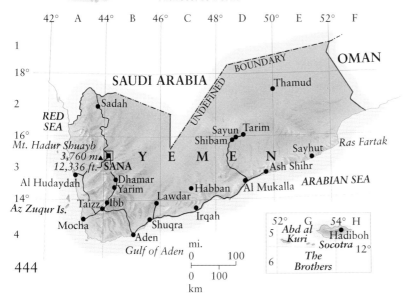

OMAN

Much of Oman, which is one of the world's hottest countries, is desert. The land ranges from barren, rocky mountains in the north to the empty, rolling sands that cover the border with Saudi Arabia. Most Omanis live on the fertile coastal strip between the mountains and the sea in the north of the country and around the town of Salalah in the south. Oman also owns Musandam, the rocky peninsula overlooking busy shipping lanes between the Persian Gulf and the Arabian Sea.

Oman has an ancient sea-trading tradition and for centuries was famed for the export of frankincense, a scented gum from a desert shrub. Today many Omanis earn their living from fishing, farming or driving herds of camels, goats and horses through scrubby wasteland in search of pasture. All depend for their water on wells, some of which are fed from underground canals built hundreds of years ago.

Oman was a poor country until 1970, when Sultan Qaboos came to power. Under his rule Oman has exploited its considerable oil wealth. Some of the income from oil has been used to improve irrigation of the land and build roads, hospitals and schools.

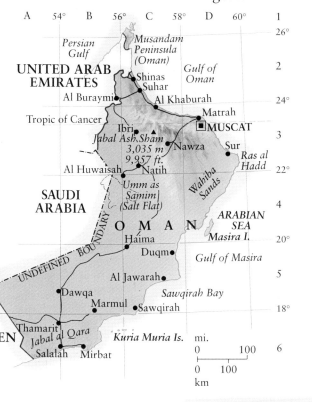

An Omani Muslim woman follows religious custom by wearing a black mask to prevent her face from being seen. She is a desert woman – city women cover only the nose, mouth and cheeks.

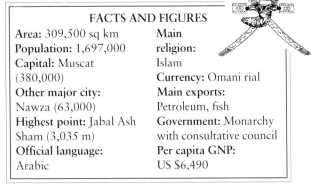

FACTS AND FIGURES

Area: 309,500 sq km
Population: 1,697,000
Capital: Muscat (380,000)
Other major city: Nawza (63,000)
Highest point: Jabal Ash Sham (3,035 m)
Official language: Arabic

Main religion: Islam
Currency: Omani rial
Main exports: Petroleum, fish
Government: Monarchy with consultative council
Per capita GNP: US $6,490

A group of fishermen launch a hand-built wooden boat. Oman has long been famous for boat building. Its large wooden sailing ships once carried cargoes along the Persian Gulf and to East Africa and India.

UNITED ARAB EMIRATES

In the early 1970s seven emirates (states ruled by emirs, or Arab princes) joined together to form the United Arab Emirates (UAE). The emirates are Abu Dhabi, Dubayy, Ash Shariqah, Ajman, Umm al Qaywayn, Ras al Khaymah and Al Fujayrah.

Until the 1900s the Arabs of this part of the Persian Gulf were seafarers. Some traded in perfumes and silk. Others were pirates and smugglers, fighting over shiploads of pearls, spices and slaves. In 1820 Britain, a strong trading power in the Persian Gulf, forced the emirates to sign a truce. They gave up warfare at sea in return for British protection. However, the emirates continued to fight each other over boundary disputes and fishing rights up until the mid-1900s, when oil brought wealth to the region.

The UAE is a barren expanse of sandy desert rising to rocky mountains in the east. Salt marshes and swamps line the coast. Before oil was discovered most people lived by diving for pearls, fishing, growing dates or herding camels. Today the majority of people live in cities and work in the oil and construction industries. Profits from oil have been used to build roads and improve healthcare and education.

▲ *Dubayy creek curves through the modern city. Dubayy is the most important commercial centre and port in the United Arab Emirates.*

FACTS AND FIGURES

Area: 83,660 sq km
Population: 1,206,000
Capital: Abu Dhabi (363,000)
Other major cities: Dubayy (585,000), Al Ayn (176,000)
Highest point: Jabal Yibir (1,527 m)

Official language: Arabic
Main religion: Islam
Currency: Dirham
Main export: Petroleum, natural gas, fish, dates
Government: Monarchy, union of emirates
Per capita GNP: US $22,220

◀ *Jockeys, many of them young boys, urge their racing camels to run faster. Camel racing is a popular sport in the United Arab Emirates. Racing camels are specially bred for speed and are highly prized.*

QATAR

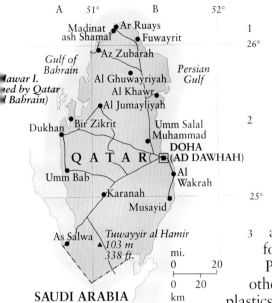

A 51° B 52°

Madinat ash Shamal
Ar Ruays
Fuwayrit
Az Zubarah
Gulf of Bahrain
Persian Gulf
Hawar I. (used by Qatar and Bahrain)
Al Ghuwayriyah
Al Khawr
Al Jumayliyah
Dukhan
Bir Zikrit
Umm Salal Muhammad
DOHA (AD DAWHAH)
Q A T A R
Umm Bab
Al Wakrah
Karanah
Musayid
As Salwa
Tuwayyir al Hamir
▲103 m
338 ft.

mi.
0   20
0   20
km

SAUDI ARABIA

1
26°

2

25°

3

Qatar

United Arab Emirates

The small peninsula of Qatar sticks up like a thumb into the Persian Gulf. Qatar was protected first by its neighbour Bahrain and then by Britain before becoming an independent emirate (ruled by a prince) in 1971. It is mainly stony desert with barren salt flats in the south. Before oil was discovered in 1939 most people survived by pearl diving, fishing and camel herding. Today 90 percent of the population are city-dwellers. Most live in or near Doha, the capital, working in oil or related industries. Plentiful jobs and good pay have attracted workers from other Arab countries and from India and Pakistan. There are now three foreigners to every native Qatari.

Profits from oil in Qatar are being used to develop other industries such as fish-freezing, fertilizers and plastics. Oil money also provides free education, free healthcare and housing for the poor. Drinking water used to come from natural springs or wells, but now Qatar has built large desalination plants where seawater is distilled to remove the salt. The fresh water is then piped to homes and used to irrigate crops. The government also helps farmers to grow more vegetables, fruit and grain by supplying them with free seeds, pesticides and fertilizers.

▶ Wooden slats in this wind tower catch the wind and funnel it down to the building below. This simple air conditioning system was developed in ancient times and is still used in modern Qatari buildings.

FACTS AND FIGURES
Area: 11,440 sq km
Population: 559,000
Capital: Doha (236,000)
Other major city: Al Wakrah (26,000)
Highest point: Tuwayyir al Hamir (103 m)
Official language: Arabic
Main religion: Islam
Currency: Qatari riyal
Main exports: Petroleum, fertilizers
Government: Constitutional monarchy (emir is head of state)
Per capita GNP: US $16,240

447

BAHRAIN

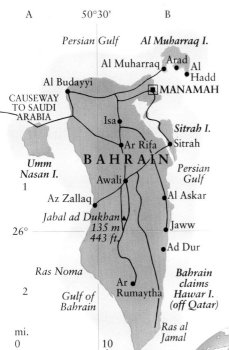

A 50°30' B

Persian Gulf **Al Muharraq I.**

Al Muharraq Arad Al
Hadd
Al Budayyi ☐MANAMAH
CAUSEWAY
TO SAUDI
ARABIA Isa
Sitrah I.
Ar Rifa Sitrah
B A H R A I N *Persian
Gulf*
*Umm
Nasan I.* Awali
1
Az Zallaq Al Askar
Jabal ad Dukhan
135 m Jaww
26° *443 ft.*
Ad Dur
Ras Noma *Bahrain
claims
Ar Hawar I.
2 Rumaytha (off Qatar)*
*Gulf of
Bahrain*
*Ras al
Jamal*
mi.
0 10
0 10
km *Ras al
Barr*

FACTS AND FIGURES
Area: 690 sq km
Population: 521,000
Capital: Manamah
(152,000)
Other major city:
Al Muharraq (78,000)
Highest point:
Jabal ad Dukhan
(135 m)
Official language: Arabic
Main religion: Islam
Currency:
Bahraini dinar
Main exports:
Petroleum, aluminium
products, manufactured
goods, machinery,
transport equipment
Government:
Monarchy (emir is
head of state)
Per capita GNP:
Est. US $3,000-8,000

Bahrain consists of about 30 islands, most of which are uninhabited desert. The largest island, also called Bahrain, is rocky and barren in the south, but in the north plentiful springs have greened the land. Bridges join the main islands and a causeway links Bahrain Island to Saudi Arabia.

Most Bahrainis are Muslim Arabs and live in the fertile north of the largest island. Traditional occupations include fishing, pearl diving, tending animals and growing fruits such as pomegranates and figs on irrigated land. Since the discovery of oil in 1932 many people have taken jobs in the petroleum industry and live in or near the capital. About one fifth of the population are immigrant workers, mainly from Pakistan and India. Oil money provides free healthcare and education. It also finances the development of new industries such as aluminium processing.

Bahrain's position in the Persian Gulf made it an important trading nation in ancient times. Today it is a thriving financial centre. During its long history Bahrain has been invaded by the Portuguese, Persians and mainland Arabs. Britain handled the country's defence and foreign affairs from 1861 until 1971, when Bahrain became independent.

▶ *Burning gases from oil wells blacken the sky of Bahrain. The country has less oil than most Gulf states, but its oil refinery is one of the biggest and most modern in the world.*